EVOL
THE SPIRIT

FROM DEMOCRACY TO PEACE

CHANGING THE WORLD IN TEN STEPS

ANTHONY RUSSELL

"All major religious traditions carry basically the same message,
that is love, compassion and forgiveness.
The important thing is they should be part of our daily lives"

The Dalai Llama

Evolving The Spirit - From Democracy to Peace
First Edition
Published by DreamStar Books, January 2012
ISBN: 978-1-904166-39-9
EAN: 9781904166399

Tel: 0870 777 3339
e-mail: info@dreamstarbooks.com

Set in 'Times'

(Font size with consideration for those preferring larger print)

Front cover photo; Bagan, Burma, taken by the author

Printed and bound in Great Britain by Imprint Digital, Devon, England

For Allegra Darwin

And the contribution of her ancestors
to the foundations of modern civilization.

Best wishes

Anthony Russell

*"A nation's culture resides in the hearts
and in the soul of its people"*

Mohandas Gandhi

*"All through this hour Lord, be my guide,
and by Thy power, no foot shall slide"*

WESTMINSTER CHIMES

*"Evolving the Spirit is a serious and thoughtful work about conflict,
leadership and the importance of forgiveness and it deserves and I
hope reaches, a wide audience"*
Tony Benn (former secretary of state & democracy campaigner)

"Your words are moving and a masterpiece"
Mike Blissett (life-skills guru)

*"Your book alerts the world to one of the finest sources of inspiration
the world has ever seen"*
Alan Clements (founder of 'World Dharma')

"I don't have a faith but your book has changed my life"
Chris Darwin (conservationist & g-g-grandson of Charles Darwin)

"Best of luck with the research and the book"
William Hague (UK Foreign Secretary.)

"Remarkable and heartening stuff"
John Simpson (BBC World Affairs Editor)

"A challenge to the way most people in the world think and act, this book sets out personal precepts for a life well lived and a world that is gentler, kinder and more just."
Peter Tatchell (human rights activist)

"I welcome this book. It is a fine exploration of a dimension that is all too frequently overlooked in the Western world; that of the human spirit. This timely book gives voice to the growing awareness today that to create a deeper democracy and a more peaceful world, matters of heart and spirit must take centre stage, both in private and public spheres. It is my hope that it will stimulate a wider debate and foster positive change."
Jane Ozanne (founder of 'Spirit of Peace')

"In this gem of a guide, Russell encourages us to know that we are not alone on our journey. I commend it to all who seek personal development and who are part of the emerging global community, determined to build a better world."
Professor Julia Häusermann MBE (founder of Rights and Humanity)

FOREWORD

It is an extraordinary privilege to have been invited to write this forward having only just met the author, Anthony Russell. But from our first telephone call a couple of weeks ago it was obvious that we shared an analysis of the myriad and interrelated challenges facing humanity and the approach that is required. It is clear to us both, as it has been to many others before us, that we are experiencing a crisis of the spirit. A new paradigm is required if we are to overcome the greed and exploitation characterising the profit-driven model of capitalism, materialism and destruction of our natural environment. We both recognise that in shaping this paradigm, the wisdoms of all of the world's main faiths and philosophies have their part to play.

I was therefore delighted when Anthony rearranged his schedule to participate last week in a gathering to mark the 25th Anniversary of Rights and Humanity, the international not-for-profit organisation which I founded in 1986, on international Human Rights Day, 10th December. Our gathering brought together a group of likeminded individuals committed to global justice, peace and sustainability. Together we adopted a Call for Action, setting out a new paradigm, based on cooperation and respect and committed ourselves to living by a few simple principles, which resonate with those espoused by Anthony in this profound book.

If I have learnt anything over the last 25 years it is that we need a change of heart and mind, a 'revolution of the spirit' as Aung

San Sui Kyi has put it. To live by our principles we need to foster our inner spiritual journey. This powerful book provides a simple path to help us on this journey of the soul, backed up with wisdom distilled down the ages from the world's main faiths and philosophies. In it Anthony combines age old adages such as 'count your blessings' with some profound new insights about the nature of the human spirit and what it means to be truly human.

In the early chapters of the book Anthony leads us through the steps we need to take to build the firm roots within ourselves to prepare us to work for peace from an energised place within. I have long had a plaque over my desk with the words "Be still and know that I am God". It is a continuous reminder to honour silence, so Anthony's starting point of experiencing what he terms 'the gap', whether through stillness, meditation or prayer, struck a deep chord in me. For many years I was rushing around the world, influencing global policy and practice and realised that I had become a 'human doing'. Over the last decade in particular, I have invested more time on nurturing myself as a 'human being', so that my inner peace might direct my doing. I wish I had had Anthony's book to guide me on this journey.

In reading *"Evolving the Spirit"* I was struck by the parallels between Anthony's steps and the insights that I have gained through Rights and Humanity's work over the last quarter decade. I believe that I can say, with confidence, that my experience demonstrates that Anthony's approach is effective. His understanding of respectful giving and the mutual benefits, which arise as much to the giver as receiver, ties in with our own understanding that respecting the human rights and dignity of anyone, enhances the dignity of humanity as a whole since, as John Donne reminds us "No man is an island entire of itself..." Further, Anthony's plea that respect for everyone should take precedence over the judgement of others, is well borne out by Rights and Humanity's experience that respectful and constructive dialogue is vastly more effective than condemnation in leading progress in policy and practice.

Anthony considers that 'forgiving', a fundamental tenet of all the major world faiths, "should be honoured as an all-powerful force for good". It was at this point in the book that I reflected on the vital aspect of self-forgiveness. For many of us, self-forgiveness might be seen as both a pre-requisite and an outcome of the steps towards personal development described in the book. Those who lack self forgiveness may find it difficult to achieve peace in silence and meditation, and so I began to consider the steps set out in the book not simply as linear, but as cyclical. The lessons learnt on each step of the journey will enhance and strengthen the continued practice of the earlier steps. As Anthony remarks, each of the steps "represents a single spirit that incorporates forgiving, resolving and healing, so that each is connected, united and working as one."

As readers we are called to rise to our own individual leadership roles, promoting a mature approach of right relations, and warned that leadership for change requires us to put our heads above the parapet. My own experience has indicated the loneliness that can accompany leadership for change and yet I believe that there are millions of us all around the world who are committed to working for justice, peace and sustainability. We need to connect and to support each other in this noble endeavour. In this gem of a guide, Anthony encourages us to know that we are not alone on our journey. I commend it to all who seek personal development and who are part of the emerging global community, determined to build a better world.

Anthony has written a book that touches people of all faiths and those with none. He expounds the strength of co-operation and of resolving issues in a non-violent manner, quoting the truth spoken by the Buddha in the fifth century BC, "Hatred does not cease by hatred, but only by love". He has been careful to balance the references to spiritual teachings and profound thinkers from around the world, and I trust that I am not upsetting this balance by ending with a Christian prayer, which has been my constant guide over many years. For me, it sums up perfectly the spiritual awakening that Anthony is nurturing as a tool for peace.

> Lord, make me an instrument of your peace;
> where there is hatred, let me sow love;
> when there is injury, pardon;
> where there is doubt, faith;
> where there is despair, hope;
> where there is darkness, light;
> and where there is sadness, joy.
> Grant that I may not so much seek
> to be consoled as to console;
> to be understood, as to understand,
> to be loved as to love;
> for it is in giving that we receive,
> it is in pardoning that we are pardoned,
> and it is in dying that we are born to eternal life (a)

Professor Julia Häusermann MBE   13 December, 2011

Founder and President of Rights and Humanity
The International Centre of Excellence in Human Rights
and Responsibilities (www.rightsandhumanity.org)

A Desert Called Peace

In the war on fear, everyone's a loser.
Violence for violence, eyes for eyes.
Blind reaction for measured action,
And a cruel lashing out in ignorance.

A blood splattered politics of spin,
Sees only self righteous democratisation.
A creeping liberty of vice,
That condemns all creeds but it's own.

We live lives superior in ability to hurt:
Charitable to the point of cruelty.
Crashing through time, pendulum swinging,
Only extremes by fear determined;

Terrorism, genocide, hunger, recession,
Armed with paranoia the damage is done.
Full swing of junk-food savagery,
Too clever to see the sense beyond,

Leaving wastelands for the helpless,
Minefields for the children,
Poverty for whole nations,
And a desert called peace.

Truly a Pax Romana!

03.05.02 (b)

" . . for the first time in history, the physical survival of the human race depends on radical change of the human heart"

"As long as everybody wants to have more,
there must be formation of classes,
there must be class war,
and in global terms there must be international war.
Greed and peace preclude each other"

ERICH FROMM

CONTENTS

BACKCLOTH

"Shiva's dance is the dance of subatomic matter"(1)

We live in a crazy world of apparently fast diminishing certainties. We know we feel, we know we will probably die in pain but the rest seems thousands of years of brave attempts to make sense of the senseless. We come naked into this world and each according their own, fights the loneliness of a lifetime; some seeking out meaning, others never needing to bother. Empires come and empires go, great movements and their apostles postulate and are discredited. We grow, we learn, we struggle, we fall asleep and are forgotten under the layers of time; millions of years; millions of tiny creatures writhing to the dance of life.

It's hard to imagine another period when so much former meaning and hope has been rendered invalid for so much of the world's population. In the march of Western civilisation *"Where wealth accumulates and men decay,"*(2) great technological advancement comes at the cost of the simple and meaningful, lost in the 'wake'. Even with a modern global lingua franca and all our communication wizardry, the story of Babel may yet come to pass, as the occupants of a great monolith lose the simple ability to communicate. Thankfully, this is not a universal predicament and the grubby faces of the materially deprived in traditional cultures challenge us with their shining warmth and love.

Many sense that unmentioned universal truths do exist to underpin life's complexities with a single thread of meaning and hope; that there really are constant beliefs, common to all the main faiths of the world if we choose to recognise them. But these are most clearly articulated at their conception, before politics and inertia, cloud the creed with fashion and prejudice. From heroic single voice to polytheistic mass worship, the gradual inclination of civilisations has been towards a constant watering down of complex truths into manageable platitudes. It has never been more imperative to undertake the re-evaluation that brings us back to those simple and timeless understandings. Should we not stand alone, a prophet in the wilderness, as many have before, against the oppressive heat of corruption in all its forms?

———————

PREFACE

*"We do not need to proselytise
either by our speech or by our writing.
We can only do so really with our lives.
Let our lives be open books for all to study"*(3)

Life is in flux. We don't understand the world till we appreciate that it is constantly changing. Without changing we are out of step with its rhythms and will inevitably decay. It is as a sailing ship that must consider the constant fluctuations of the wind with regular trimming of the sails or languish in the doldrums. And it is for example, why governing bodies of sports need to consider rule changes, as skills improve and styles change.

In the same way, we need to constantly adapt to new situations with fresh methods and approaches. That is both the challenge and the excitement of living life to the full. Life is also full of examples where *form* has not kept pace with *content,* or if you like, where the method has not kept up with the purpose. Democracy is a fragile bloom and corruption is sadly not confined to distant banana republics. It is too easy for power once residing in time-honoured institutions to slip quietly away and leave those still noisy bodies relatively powerless. Likewise, many a noble and wise utterance has become meaningless over time and the perfect kernel of *content* has been lost in a meaningless elaboration of *form*. While it is true that 'political incorrectness' can typify indifference and cause real offence, content can leave the 'correct' form at will, rendering 'PC' language quite meaningless. It is the content, in other words; the spirit behind any gesture, that should be judged over the form it takes.

While it is true that commerce driven cultures are concerned with change, it is generally only with the *form* and seldom the meaning behind it. Constant fluctuations; so called *progress* and *change* have become modern obsessions for their own sake and as a by-product of capitalism. There is a blind adherence to the benefits of constant change and what is imagined to be the 'healthy march of civilisation towards a freer and richer life'. But drowning in the wake of this obsession is any understanding of more constant cultures surviving today or forgotten in our history. Much of the past is now deemed simply backward and as a memory of needless suffering. While acknowledging the comforts of modernity, out with the water went the baby of a slower, more contemplative life with any reassuring constants, not just of dependable communities but also constant understandings. Alongside ancient superstition was also a subtle nuance to much interpretation, hard for a modern, invariably darting mind to comprehend. No one would sensibly advocate regressing to former ages of supposed innocence, nor the renouncing of hard won change and progress. But it is important to step outside our hectic lives, take the time to realise that despite the constant change, there are constants that never change. Taking the opportunity, we can appreciate certain truths that when spoken, immediately ring true within us, as if they came from deep within an understanding and had been forgotten or suppressed. *"All know the way, but few actually walk it."*(4)

My intention in this book is to reiterate and clarify these truths. Though I may cherish them they are of course not mine. In fact, a *ten steps to enlightenment* was written by the Japanese monk Kutai twelve centuries ago.(5) But to my mind, this revelation only proves their timelessness as the free inheritance of all. I will support and evaluate them as they unfold but without writing volumes of supporting evidence. These are powerful truths that stand on their own merit in our appreciation. They are what the American Constitution would call "*self-evident*"(6) or as Gandhi put it; ". . . a*s soon as you remove the cobwebs of ignorance that surround it, (the truth) shines clear.*"(7) We say *'don't blame the messenger'*; but I would say, don't judge the prophecy by the prophet. Implicit in this statement is the warning never to accept other's opinions at face value. No one is infallible and every utterance must have that ring of truth, while at the same time be submitted to the laws of experience and common sense.

Also, while I will constantly quote others much wiser than myself, in this book specific expertise is less relevant to my task. Our greatest tool to understanding the truth within these pages is through a life rich in its variety. It is this experience that I claim as my mandate. Another casualty of lives obsessed with commerce, is the worship of the specialist; the 'expert', with the skills to make money. Where there is mass production, there is a need for specific disciplines, from the simplest cog on the factory floor to the emeritus professor. But this imperative has seen the demise of the polymath, the Renaissance Man, the amateur. With it we have lost the understanding of wisdom, defined as breadth of knowledge. The very word amateur has become debased and yet it is the amateur and the polymath who will think outside the box. One need only recall Leonardo da Vinci, possibly the last man to know everything or Charles Darwin to make the point. To gain in wisdom, it is therefore vital to buck the trend towards specialisation and constantly broaden the mind. Materialism can erode wisdom and impoverish us as a result. I could ask myself why it has taken so many years to set aside the time to write these pages. It appears I had not previously allowed myself the 'indulgence'. Perhaps my growing years of experience have given me the maturity to recognise my instincts at last. After all, the freedom to pursue a personal dream is surely the hope of all civilisation.

It is not my intention to undertake a lengthy anti-capitalist rant. Only a true hypocrite would sit before his computer in twenty first century comfort and condemn it outright. However, while democracy is arguably *'the best system we have'*,(8) we should not blindly accept it as synonymous with modern commerce. In fact commerce has proved a tyrant, constantly threatening democratic rule. This dictator exerts power not only directly, through the influence of politics and wealth but also subliminally, in the gradual indoctrination of generations. A sophisticated culture of deception has crept unnoticed into a society that can no longer discern clearly and is left profoundly compromised. In reality, the interests of commerce and the individual are often in conflict, nowhere more so than in the desperate struggle to preserve the ecology of this planet. Free-market capitalism is now widely seen as a direct obstacle to tackling most of the pressing human issues we face today; what economists call *"Market Failure."*(9) This phenomenon is creating a profound dichotomy within the collective conscience and with it a kind of hell on earth. Many forms of related schizoid behaviours are producing deep confusion in the modern mind, often only touched on in the mystery of dreams. Therefore, any path out of such a hell, towards the goal of peace, must confront this great dichotomy.

The 'market' has truly failed us because it has taken the 'spirit' or spiritual out of life and left us with a suspicion for anything that is not a commodity for sale. Unfortunately love is not a commodity and so has suffered as a result and left us all the poorer in our wealth. Anything without a price and therefore in-exchangeable is rendered worthless and nothing is left sacred. In the words of E F Schumacher; *". . . if economic thinking pervades the whole of society, even simple non economic values like beauty, health or cleanliness can survive only if they prove to be 'economic'"*.(10)

I should perhaps warn that ultimately there is a sting in the tail of this beast of mine. The first step is difficult but the last may well prove the hardest for many to accept. It is as controversial and threatening today as it was in Roman times though just as relevant. Those recognising it are still pilloried and some 'crucified' for it. But such strong reactions have always been considered the proof of its validity and the fear such truth can provoke.

I talk of simple truths and they are best served by a simple format. As well as a cover-to-cover read, I want to provide easy reference for those preferring to dip in. I have therefore formulated ten steps to give the impression of a journey upward and out of the darkness of misunderstanding and confusion. It is a stepped path out of what I see as a kind of hell, where hell takes the form perhaps always intended, not a remote place of the future but beyond the constraints of our time-bound world; a spirit, a state of mind and the opposite of the Buddhist notion of *nirvana*.(11) But with the steps, I also had in mind to echo perhaps the disciplined approach of the *Minnesota Method*.(12)

I intend to give simple reassurance to those for whom such truth is obvious and I feel no need to apologise for that. Equally, I hope to offer guidance for the many who crave the essential role models to make sense of life. This audience is just as likely to be a parent as the young and is possibly both. I also appreciate that true understanding comes from living not words; that is to say, through the spirit within, rather than manifested in an action or utterance. If you like, exactly the opposite of the expression *"do as I say, not as I do."*(13) Those who think children will believe their parents, simply by the spoken word, constantly underestimate the young. Nature makes children acutely aware of the inner 'spirit' of their parents as an essential means of survival. This makes children the masters in understanding the sub-plot that reveals actual intent.

It is painfully obvious to us in this day and age as much as any other, that there are many for whom no message of hope will penetrate their damaged consciousness. Violence and conflict are all they know and a madness dictates their every action. Individuals and nations face immediate threats and with the best will to nurture a culture of peace, 'fire-fighting' containment is sometimes the only option. I recognise this as I also appreciate the need for compromise and the realities of political engagement in a real world. But these are obstacles rather than arguments against the basic principles set out in these pages. The culture of conflict that has resulted in so much insanity is the issue here and a healthy 'culture' will inevitably take time to grow in the 'gut' of humanity.

So I write this to simply support the binding truth revealed by all-important experience, trusting that my words will ring true, give comfort and perhaps echo in the mind of the child I never had.

*"People today are yearning for human beings
who have wisdom and conviction and the courage to act
according to their convictions"*(14)

———————

STEP 1

THE GAP

"Where there is nothing, there is God"(15)

The first step is the most abstract and therefore perhaps the most challenging. For that reason it needs forbearance as we suspend preconceptions, exercise the mind and go with the flow.

Biologists declare that every one of us is an evolutionary success story; millions of years of fruitful procreation as the miraculous survivors of an incredible food chain. So whoever is reading this is one of nature's winners. We should perhaps be able to naturally empathise with hapless old families, no longer able to manage ancient ancestral piles following a long line of tradition. For *our* winning ancestors go back millions of years and to forgo having children is to break that chain with an end to the great line.

Science has brought us obvious benefits; the 'miracle' of penicillin fostered generations of strict adherents committed to its ascendancy. But any historian will counter that despite the discipline of empirical research, science has constantly contradicted itself. Respect for its phenomenal achievements in the

1

face of ignorance and exploitation, needs to be balanced with a healthy scepticism. Despite its most rigorous endeavours, market forces as well as political and dogmatic imperatives have regularly compromised genuine research. Science's greatest value is as a tool to understanding rather than a 'religion' in its own right or what William James called *scientificism*.(16)

While science has been valuable in checking the excesses of religion, it has proved itself a bad substitute, apparently unable to answer the questions that matter most to humans. It is also argued, that far from the panacea once envisaged, science has reeked as much havoc as it provided sustainable solutions. Old diseases have resurged; pesticides increased pest numbers and environmental poisoning; the soil depleted and hi-tech human environments increased unemployment and stress levels.(17) For one example, consider the promise of Henry Kissinger in 1974 that "*within a decade, no man, woman or child will go to bed hungry*". Now, over three decades later, the number of hungry people in the world has doubled to almost a billion. While admittedly political issues play their part, technical advance has failed to provide workable solutions. It appears the more we rely on science alone to answer our most personal needs, the more fruitless it proves. In the end, it is perhaps wiser to admit our fallibility, accept that limitations to life do exist and see it ultimately as; ". . . *a mystery to be lived, not a problem to be solved.*"(18)

In what, therefore, can we put our trust that is not scientifically proven? One could equally reverse the inference and demand of science of what the universe is made and what is beyond it? Or how does gravity work? Is time an illusion? Why do placebos work? Many questions are worth asking precisely because they appear unanswerable. By the same token, because something cannot be scientifically proven it doesn't mean it doesn't exist or is invalid. This is a truism for scientists and those suspicious of it alike. The risk is that blindness to scientifically proven phenomena by religious extremism could drive science into an entrenched position. From there, it is less open to the kind of imaginative thinking that has often inspired the scientific discoveries we accept as fact today. As it is humans that undertake scientific research, it is human understanding and intention that must inevitably limit it. In the words of Bertrand Russell; *"Science may set limits to knowledge, but should not set limits to imagination."*(19)

For example, as an exercise, try to grapple with the notion of eternity, the beginning or end of time, space or mass. We soon realise that much is still entirely beyond the realms of scientific understanding because it is beyond the finite human brain. There may therefore be other ways of interpreting the world around us that can complement science, rather than fly in the face of it. We have specific understandings of the world in the scriptures of the various religions. The Bible, for example, appears to the uninitiated as an unequivocal document of fact, where a lot of it can seem simply outrageous. On closer inspection, the Bible can be seen to conflict with itself, if read in strictly literal terms. It suffers today because its tales are seen as ancient and ignorant superstition, when considered out of the context that gives it power. It should more accurately be interpreted as a work of art, with perhaps the Creation, as its most imaginative masterpiece. Art penetrates the truth and moves us with its mystery, so why not scripture?

There has also been a serious risk within the separation of science and art, for it has lead to the misunderstanding of both. It is important to differentiate between the form and content of art. We are aware of the difference between plot and theme in a novel or between the implausible librettos and powerful emotions evident in opera. But as in the Bible, to fixate on the plot, is to miss the spirit it lives to convey. Our empirical age has lost us the ability to interpret much around us. We vaguely understand that there is more to Greek mythology than improbable stories or that seventeenth century Dutch genre painting had meaning beyond the loving rendition of everyday objects.(20) But there is a risk of labelling anything we hold precious, that is not verified by the scientific establishment, as *"petty private beliefs."*(21) We are at least, all too aware today that information is not in itself meaning; that interpretation requires more than facts and figures and that this requires an element of letting go; of having *faith*. When the composer and visionary Sir John Tavener's music was accused of having no substance, he responded; *"but I'm not interested in substance, it's the essence of the music that counts!"* (22)

The word faith here is being used with an emphatically small 'f', for throughout the world, peoples of different 'Faiths', have nevertheless shared 'faith'. In the broadest sense faith is the assurance that the sun will rise in the morning, that the sky will not fall on our heads, that there is goodness in the world and love in abundance. This realisation transcends individual religions, is the basis of hope and the foundation of love. It also indicates cohesion between religions often overlooked in the sectarian's effort to highlight their differences. We must not forget that the origin of the word religion; *re-ligãre* as about uniting and bringing together.

So far we have considered a series of breaches or common misunderstandings resulting in and from social polarisation. It is hardly surprising if much of the world has become factionalised in its thinking when much of it adheres to the principles of adversarial democracy. This is as true for politics and the law, as it is for sport and the media. The brevity forced on us by competitive commerce, demands the briefest of sound-bites. This in turn precludes the detailed response that complex questions usually require. As a result, simplistic attitudes and positions have become rooted in our culture. There is therefore a need to step back and revalue, in tandem with science and common sense and using a simple practical approach. The aim after all is to climb that first step and to do it, let us employ an exercise we'll call the *'Gap Theory'*. Mentally it requires an element of 'going with the flow' and for many this will prove a challenge but consider it a warm-up exercise to open the mind for the climb ahead.

You get the sense these days that to an increasing extent science is also going with the flow. Discoveries have become so implausibly beyond normal comprehension, that in attempting to understand the world around us, a new kind of openness is required. This is surely good news and has resulted in scientists using biblical terms to describe the latest understanding. This is also helping to restore the unity lost in the division of human thought, particularly between science and the arts. For example the discovery that types of elements run in scales of seven, has made a fascinating parallel with the seven notes of an octave. This creates a significant 'gap' and is arguably mirrored by science proposing the universe to be constructed of black holes. It is possible that all we yearn to know lies within that gap. Perhaps Londoners should be grateful that every time they get on the Underground they are reminded to mind it. In this gap are silence, peace and nothingness, which is actually 'everythingness'. We are aware that the greatest understanding comes from silent contemplation, from doing 'nothing'. This is sometimes termed meditation or for others, devotion or prayer. We are also aware for example, that music gains its power from silence and that the gaps between the notes are accepted as of equal importance to the notes themselves. We will consider the notion of contemplation further in Step 3, as here we are more concerned with the phenomenon rather than the method. Step 1 therefore is really about 'nothing' and it is appropriate to start with nothing; a blank canvas.

The oxymoron of *'doing nothing'* is an important concept here and as a state of mind sometimes crucial. Anyone experienced in managing a crisis, will recognise that the first thing to 'do' should actually be nothing. It is understood that even if only a split second is available before something must be done, it is worth using that time to evaluate the situation. This avoids doing something inappropriate, when driven by the heat of the moment and making the situation worse. The same goes for life. Of course one should ask; when is nothing really nothing? Science tells us there must be something in a gap but of course our gap is a gap in the abstract sense, as a phenomenon, almost as an attitude or spirit.

One might find it helpful to use the analogy of life as a fast moving train. We very often have the sense that we don't remember getting on it, are not sure where it is going or how to get off. This is of course the train of our superego, the one driven by our past, our culture, our family and friends. There are other trains or means of transport that we might choose. Those who have the courage to leap from the 'Superego Train' find themselves running alongside it for a while until the existing momentum is spent. It would be wrong however to keep running, for that would probably be in the same direction and undoubtedly someone else's. No, it is vital to come to a stop and experience the *gap*. It's about stopping, feeling, sensing and evaluating before doing anything. Only then, having noticed the scenery and considered the options is it possible to proceed in an independent and self-motivated direction. As a result, the new course is invariably enlightening and deeply satisfying. Put another way, it is easy for us to arrange a holiday break that includes endless activities and worthy sites. So much is 'done' but no more is necessarily achieved than by doing 'nothing'. This nothing might involve sitting in a square having a cup of coffee watching the world go by. It might involve sitting on a remote hill observing the sun slowly set. We know from experience that these are very often the most memorable moments and possibly even the most informative.

A life experienced fully, informs us but also tells us how little we know. It is a well-known maxim that the older one gets, the more apparent this becomes. It is also said that a little knowledge is a dangerous thing but then, against the vastness of understanding, our lack of it will always be a danger. It is therefore important to temper the euphoria of knowledge with the reality of our ignorance. This is after all a basic tenet of modesty without which we *fall*.(23) It is surely as much about being open, open to new ideas and experiences, without which we cannot grow and would quickly decay.

So part of coming to terms with the world and being realistic about it, is the realisation of one's powerlessness in the face of so much that is unfathomable. When this concept is confronted, far from inducing alarm, it is actually quite liberating. This is because a lot of the psychological props and baggage associated with half-truths and false knowledge can be discarded. Each of the many languages of the world is limited by its own size. Learning a new language teaches us this, as we discover different understandings that broaden the mind. Our understanding of the world was once limited by our inability to leave it. Similarly, a tour guide who has never left their own country and having no yardstick for comparison will struggle to communicate its characteristics. Time was once considered a universal constant because there appeared no escape. Now we know that it is affected, possibly created by the mass that is our planet. It may even be a complete illusion. Though it is unfashionable to say it, much of the creative genius that forged new thinking by humans was inspired under the influence of mind-altering drugs. The risks of addiction are real but so is their capacity to free the mind from some of its many constraints.

We are taught that; *"Nature abhors a vacuum."*(24) Having accepted and come to appreciate this gap, it is inevitable that something will fill it, for such is the law of nature. Modern life crowds everything with meaning and form and itself mistrusts any kind of pause or emptiness. But this is the very reason why we need to follow the prophets into the metaphorical dessert and step aside. There is an enormous risk that this 'sacred space' can be easily filled with so much distraction and only end up distracting. For example, into our gap could be put hard work or alcohol, legal and illegal drugs, sex and much else besides. When you fight to avoid the gap by using any of these methods you are at risk of addiction and becoming a slave to them. There is only one safe way to fill the gap and that is with love.

Of course in one respect this gap is not a gap at all, it is quite the opposite, it is the very substance, the very *being* of life. But because it cannot be seen or exchanged it is not acknowledged or valued in a society that revolves around commodities. The word 'spirit' has lost its meaning to describe what we cannot see. But every culture on this earth has acknowledged in some form or other, something approximating to a 'spirit'. To understand the meaning of the word, we have to appreciate the poverty of our industrialised age that can only appreciate the material. Anything to do with experience, in other words *'Being'*, which is not quantifiable in the same sense as the material, has suffered as a result. Anything that is not a commodity and cannot be bought and valued on the market, has been diminished. The result is that words such as *spirit* have been associated with mere superstition. Rather than recognise the common spirit of love and truth that touches the breadth of humanity, religions and philosophies become separated dogmas to be challenged or traded. In *having* a religion like a possession, any other approach is attacked as wrong and any true spirit that existed within them; the spirit of *being,* is lost.

A clear explanation of the meaning of this spirit was given by the philosopher Erich Fromm in his book *'To Have or to Be?'*.(25) If you live for pleasure from the possessions you have and crave, you cannot be in the moment and are a slave to what you own. However, a spiritual life is not one entirely without possessions - for this would be difficult - but without the cravings to possess that make us identify ourselves by what we *have* and not by what we *are*. Fromm argues that this is difficult for us to appreciate because we have gone for three hundred years living to possess, to accumulate, to conquer and dominate. Not that these characteristics didn't exist before among certain sections of societies, but that now it is the dominant orientation of an industrial age of relative comfort.

Again, all the principle religions of the world acknowledged this craving and 'worship' of possessions as the great sin. They also share the belief that freedom from it is the rightful path not just to enlightenment but also lasting peace. The problem is, the insidious effects of advertising often drown out the message of true faith around the world. The propaganda of mass marketing and a pernicious media, have to a great extent confused modern societies and left them unable to think clearly. Because of the resulting insecurity; because of greed and envy, there exists a powerful drive to compete, to dominate and destroy. It exists in the minds of society's individuals as a disease that can break out into open violence at a moment's notice. The result is that so-called peacetime is sometimes considered little more than a truce and the urge to conquer others, to defeat anybody and everybody is never far away. Darwin never intended for his theory of natural selection to be taken as the justification for human selfishness and conquest. Even Richard Dawkins has admitted that his influential book *'The Selfish Gene'*, should more correctly have been entitled, *'The Immortal Gene'*.(26)

Fromm realised this was a problem of the obsession with ownership and greed, that was blinding modern man and setting him on a course for destruction: The industrial West is built on the principles of possession of private property; *"what the sources of property are does not matter; nor does possession impose any obligations on the property owner. The principle is: 'Where and how my property was acquired or what I do with it is nobody's business but my own; as long as I do not violate the law, my right is unrestricted and absolute.'"*(27) The problem with this attitude is that it allows any kind of legal abuse of individuals and the environment, without any sense of personal responsibility. But it gets worse: *"To maintain control over private property we need to use power to protect it from those who would take it from us, because they, like us, can never have enough; the desire to have private property produces the desire to use violence . . ."*(28) So there we have it, the direct link between ownership, greed and violence.

A society built and administered on the principles of ownership and greed is a risk to itself. E F Schumacher, the economist and author of 'Small is Beautiful', knew in the early 1970's where this would lead and his predictions are appearing to be accurate: *"Economy as a content of life is a deadly illness, because infinite growth does not fit into a finite world. That economy should not be the content of life has been told to mankind by all the great teachers."*(29) But nobody understood the risks better than the Nobel Peace Prize winner Albert Schweitzer; *"it is obvious to everybody that we are in a process of cultural self destruction. What is left is not secure any more". "For two or three centuries many individuals have lived only as working beings and not as human beings."*(30) No wonder so many in our society feel the helplessness and meaninglessness of their unending treadmill existence. And no wonder that disillusionment and confusion have lead to mental dysfunction, violence and suicidal tendencies in all their forms. These really were prophets in the wilderness and we now see the uncomfortable evidence of their predictions. Consider alone Fromm's concern for the effects of this violence on our environment; *" . . . the conquest (of nature) has become more and more equivalent to destruction. Our spirit of conquest and hostility has blinded us to the fact that natural resources have their limit and can eventually be exhausted, and that nature will fight back against human rapaciousness.*"(31)

Any understanding of the nature of peace must recognise this malaise and work constantly towards existing in the 'being mode'. Every step we take towards peace will bring us nearer to living in the moment, sensing the joy of genuine aliveness and having the confidence to truly love the world in every individual.

> *"See how nature - trees, flowers, grass - grows in silence;*
> *see the stars, the moon and the sun,*
> *how they move in silence ...*
> *We need silence to be able to touch souls"*(32)

STEP 2

BREATHING

"Whenever I feel blue, I start breathing again"(33)

The first step was so much theory and yet was the all-important thought coming before the action. Any discipline requires careful consideration before its application. One thinks of the artist sitting before the canvas in contemplation or the gymnast taking those critical seconds to compose the mind, before launching into a demanding routine. However, while Step 2 is a physical one with more obvious scientifically proven effects, it is as much a preparatory move as the first.

The scientific understanding around breathing is clear. Breathing slowly and deeply increases oxygen supply to the vital organs of the body and particularly the brain. We can survive for weeks without food and days without water but starved of oxygen, our brains are irreparably damaged within minutes. But breathing is also vital for the expulsion of many toxins from the body. Unfortunately, bad breath can be a common side effect and avoiding the embarrassment, can cause compromise in the quality of breathing. So vital is this gas to proper functioning, that even with slightly reduced amounts of oxygen the body will not perform as well and the brain will become sluggish and less effective. Oxygen deprivation has been associated with amongst other things; irritability, bad circulation, poor eyesight and heart disease. Oxygen also purifies the blood stream, so it is hard to imagine a single bodily function more essential to consider.

Of course there is more than simply the quality of the breathing to consider. Posture is a worthy science in its own right and also has a positive effect. I have to thank my father for his remarkably effective cure for hiccups, which appreciated the connection between breathing, posture and the mind.(34) He would advise the following; make sure you are sitting comfortably but upright in an armchair, with your head up and your hands placed on the armrests. Begin to breathe in slowly through your nose, as slowly as possible while maintaining the constant flow. Reach the very top of your breath and then without sudden movement, start the descent, breathing out through your mouth, slowly and constantly, until the very bottom of the breath is reached. Again, don't hold it there but start the controlled and constant assent again. Do this several times, until the hiccups are cured. Yes, the body is taken under control but to no less an extent is the mind, with its powerful ability to affect the body.

While the benefits of correct breathing are well understood, they are still generally undervalued. If you watch that gymnast carefully, you will note the most obvious outward action as careful, slow and regular breathing. This has the effect of increasing oxygen levels to the body but it will also have a profoundly stabilising effect on the mind and therefore as a result, on the whole body.

We perhaps more readily recognise this requirement for athletes than in our own everyday lives. Consider going to an interview for a new job. If one can concentrate on nothing else while waiting nervously to be called in before a potential new employer, careful breathing should be foremost in the mind. Ten slow, rhythmic breaths will do more than anything else to calm the mind and body. Best not overdo it though, as the rather dramatic effects of hyperventilating through excessive oxygen intake will hardly help. But calm breathing assists clear thinking and will make you feel and look more relaxed. The face will appear brighter and the voice less strained. You will act with more deliberation and with better intent and you are more likely to act rather than react. This will inevitably make you radiate more confidence and this self-confidence inspires confidence in others. All this, crucially, before you have even said a word! It needs to be considered because the first natural effect of a nervous situation is to breathe faster and more erratically and this will have a direct effect on various functions within the body.

Let us go back many millennia to our assumed origins within the trees, living on our wits to survive the constant risks from predators. The body is a sophisticated organism, with complex chemical movements for specific states of being. Our bodies functioned quite clearly in what has been acknowledged as two principle states. These are on the one hand *fight* and *flight* and on the other *eating* and *sleeping,* and are known as the sympathetic and parasympathetic modes respectively. If you are fearful, you will induce chemical changes within the body that will place you in the sympathetic mode. The most obvious chemical involved in this process is adrenalin. The body recognises that in the wild you are fearful because the brain has perceived a threat, which will consequently require the action of either fighting or running. These are the actions for example, that require large amount of blood to the limbs and adrenalin is involved in facilitating this. Conversely, if you introduce regular slow breathing, it will induce relaxation and the parasympathetic mode will take over. This is appropriate for eating, when large amounts of blood are required for digestion and after it, sleep, when the breathing is at its slowest and most constant.

This is an important science to consider because of the risks of blurring the distinctions between these states of functioning and because breathing can have a remarkably powerful affect either way. The risks are that fear can make one live permanently in the sympathetic mode, with the serious effects that food will not be properly digested and sleep will be difficult. Likewise, fear could be seen as split into two principle kinds and is more popularly termed today as 'stress'. If you like, there is the 'circumstantial stress' experienced when facing for example a charging bull. It is understandable and immediate and in fact, the body will take over pretty effectively in deciding how to act. But then there is what the existentialists would have termed *Angst*(35) or could be called 'fundamental stress'. This is a programmed state within us and the result of our individual natures but it can result in a gnawing and constant fear. This stress is much harder to pinpoint and harder to deal with but left unchecked will certainly have major debilitating effects. For example, fundamental stress might lead one to work a manic existence to escape some unseen predator or ghost. Rather than 'honouring' the body with an appropriate break for lunch, it is too easy to take food 'on the hoof', while the body is still clearly in the sympathetic mode.

In not clarifying for your body the correct mode appropriate for the moment, you risk another danger; the sacrifice of appropriate sleep. We all recognise the benefits of quality time asleep but are we always vigilant to ensure the body is clear about what it should be doing? Good breathing is one apparent message to the body that it is time to wind down and enter the rejuvenating state of deep sleep. This condition will be harder to achieve if there are fears or preoccupations on the mind. It will also not help, if one has just been in a heightened state of action or perhaps already spent too much time sleeping. Where possible, it is therefore important to clearly maintain the day for actions and the night for sleep. Regular patterns help the body find this rhythm.

It is also helpful to prepare the body for sleep. This means avoiding violent, action-filled influences both real and virtual. Reading a relaxing book in bed can help this process. The length of time asleep can be limited until a clear extent of deep sleep is achieved. For example if you are having trouble sleeping, go to bed later and get up earlier and do this regularly. Do not be tempted to sleep late or go to bed early to counteract a bad night, as this is likely to be counterproductive. Once deep sleep has been achieved, then it is possible to lengthen the time in bed. Sleeping pills in anything but extreme situations will not help, as they represent borrowed time and must be 'paid back' at some point, not to mention the confusing effect they have on the body's own mechanisms.

As in all life, it is a question of balance and the various functions of life need to be respected and monitored. You will know if the balance is lost, as would anyone who has suffered the terrible spiral of confusion that can lead to serious mental dysfunction. But many modern societies are plagued by this confusion in the mind, with its recognisable symptoms. These can then affect one's mentality and the spiral starts. Much of the obvious symptoms of this malaise, end up before the doctor, who would traditionally attempt to palliate with the latest drugs. But headaches are not caused by a lack of painkillers and the effect can be to exacerbate the body's predicament. Here is an analogy; imagine a pilot, who notices a warning light telling him his plane is running low on fuel. He would be foolish to reach for a hammer and smash the light, for it would have no effect on the result, he would simply have lost the indicator. Likewise, the body is a deeply subtle 'instrument' and if respected and listened to, will tell you much about its functioning.

There can be no quicker way to start a restorative process than by careful breathing. There is a simple treatment, which illustrates neatly the relationship between mind and body. Aromatherapy is a form of massage using essential oils. Its effect on the body is palpable and probably more complex than is readily understood. But its real power is in the effect it has on the mind. It is invariably accompanied by soft lighting and relaxing music and the combined effect is to calm the mind and restore the balance. Once the 'command centre' at the head is on board, it can effect positive changes throughout the body and that will in turn positively affect the mind. We're now moving in an upward spiral.

When the body's functions are balanced, then life can be lived to the full. This balance allows us to optimise our performance. Eat, rest, act, sleep, all these need to be respected as individual functions. For example, good quality sleep allows for better functioning when awake and to engage in life to the full *"sleep is the only proper situation for inactivity, the state of awakeness is one in which laziness should have no place."*(36) So in conclusion, breathing has a measurable effect on the body but its effect on the mind is immeasurable.

"In love's godlike breathing,
there's the innermost aspect of the universe"(37)

STEP 3

LISTENING

Beyond the spectrum is what we do not see(38)

The first step might have bewildered and the second required careful application. The third will certainly need discipline but will reward us with obvious benefits in our everyday lives. Listening has the potential to be an awesome power, far more proactive than often appreciated and seldom fully valued. However, much of the discipline required will have to do with applying restraint and subtle powers of observation.

Let us consider the nature of listening. We live in an age dominated by vision. Clear evidence of this is the somewhat incongruous word *'audience'* given to theatre or cinemagoers. In Shakespeare's time, the act of listening dominated any visual effect on the stage. There certainly was not the same preoccupation with visual realism and the words were paramount in conveying a scene.

And there are problems with the modern bias towards visual stimulation. For one thing, we tend to see too much in terms of its outward form, allowing it to become a symbol of the truth within. Too easily we forget that form is a 'form' of illusion and that the truth will have only briefly passed through that form and moved on. The biblical abhorrence of the worship of *graven images*(39) is recognition of this risk. Another problem is that most of the world - the reality we know about - is hidden from our vision, making sight a very limited tool for understanding everything around us. For example we see seven colours in the spectrum and miss just off the scales at either end, ultraviolet and infrared. But we are aware that beyond them is a possibly infinite range about which we know very little. Likewise our vision is set to operate within a limited scale and speed. But we now realise that much of reality is too small for us to observe and faster or slower than we can see or comprehend. The latter becomes apparent for example when plant growth is speeded up to reveal an entirely different dimension to existence.

The dominance of vision over the other senses has gone hand in hand with our increasing preoccupation with the material; the tangible, if you like. Neglected, the other senses can catch us by surprise. Thoughts can come to mind apparently from nowhere but may well be triggered by a remembered smell or sound; deeply subtle but just beyond the reach of our cognitive mind. Not of course, that the modern material world avoids sound, in fact we are bombarded by it. It is natural for those brought up in an environment of constant noise to accept it as normal and feel deprived when it is absent. But like fear of the dark, this can be a fear of yourself, fear of the truth.

The more we hear the less we listen. There is here an important truth about our senses and the way we relate to the world around us. When you tap your finger you feel the sense but repeated tapping will deaden that sensation. This reality is equally true for sound, as we know music gets its power from silence. We are all aware of the increased awareness caused by sexual abstinence or the lessening effects of drugs from prolonged use. All sensations are as the release of an electric charge; when something is given away, the intensity is reduced. We should therefore protect our senses in order to maintain their potency. Advocating sensual 'abstinence' may sound somewhat puritanical but it is an unavoidable fact of life. This is a cautionary note worth remembering but also the key to understanding life's experiences.

Constant audio or visually intense environments create an artificial bubble, separating us from what is natural and deadening our ability to perceive and process the world around us. In other words, we are distracted and our concentration shattered in all directions. There may be circumstances when such a state is appropriate but it will not allow for the dedicated application so important to healthy living, besides which, it can become dangerously addictive.

Concentration is a great art and vital to success in any endeavour. This is usually understood in the work-place, although there can be plenty of distractions provided, often to counteract the endless monotony of many jobs. But any understanding of the need for concentration is often abandoned in the home environment. The best example of this is a household that leaves a television on all day, regardless of the presence of visitors. Clear, meaningful, communication requires the minimum of distractions. How can you listen or be heard properly while there is conflicting stimuli in the room with you? Besides which, it is well understood by the media that visual stimuli tends to dominate sound in such circumstances, which is why the images on a television will constantly change, providing a flickering distraction. Of course, there are many unavoidable distractions in life, such as the presence of young children but they don't alter the principle or the effect. A clear understanding of the requirement for concentration in everyday life was beautifully articulated by the philosopher Erich Fromm; *"If one is after quick results, one never learns an art. Yet, for modern man, patience is as difficult to practice as discipline and concentration."*(40)

Let's assume you are in possession of the luxury of this quality time with another person. Step 1 suggested the significance of restraint, that is to say, the need to do nothing first. This is the foundation stone of the art of listening. We all need to talk, that is accepted. Often we are asked to communicate information and there is no meaningful communication without dialogue. But the healthiest communication puts a strong emphasis on listening. This appears much easier to do if you have been in a quiet state alone before meeting anyone, so first we should consider the art of silent reflection, as the perfect pre-meeting exercise. *"Sometimes one creates a dynamic impression by saying something, and sometimes one creates as significant an impression by remaining silent."*(41)

Step 2 was about the importance of breathing for the proper function of the body and particularly the mind. We can now use that 'centeredness' to help achieve our listening goals. Listening in the broadest sense of the word is the main concern of the reflective state. One could call it meditation or prayer but this would be to suggest adherence to specific religious creeds that are not our concern here. Here we are considering the state these different religions all recognise as crucial in the form of *exercises* or states of being. They may call them different names and approach them with some variation but in essence they are the same phenomenon, not so much an act as a state of existence. You may not adhere to the specific creeds but it is hard to deny the wisdom of this approach.

So what is this approach? One could consider this formula: self-control, leading to self-understanding and self-enlightenment, resulting in an altered perspective, changed actions and therefore altered effect. One can deduce therefore, that from simple self-control, it is possible to clearly affect the world around us. It just seems a contradiction that holding back could be so positive. Put another way, by stepping aside and reflecting, by sharpening our awareness of the world around us, we gain greatly and can effect worthwhile change. It is sometimes argued that real power resides in the unused potential, while the spent, kinetic energy is merely wasted.

Consider two practical approaches to this, the Buddhist and the Christian. The Buddhist strives to sit in quiet meditation. It's not a thinking state. On the contrary, it is about emptying the mind, using devices such as good breathing. By overcoming absorption with oneself - the *ego* - one gains a state of heightened awareness and a calm that balances the whole body. Buddhism understands that this open state of being, without action, brings one closer to enlightenment and true understanding. Of course, with understanding one's subsequent actions are better placed and more appropriate.

In *prayer*, other 'Faiths' believe almost exactly the same principle but using a different language. Unfortunately much modern Christian practice has been corrupted, so that there is a popular belief that prayer is about speaking with God and asking him to *intercede* on our behalf. This is clearly nonsense as the origins of the word intercession are far subtler. It comes from the Latin *inter-cede*; to go amongst or alongside.(42) This suggests togetherness and mutuality rather than an imposition or conflict.

With Christianity, it is God one gets closer to and therefore his personification as love.(43) The Christian doesn't pray for things to happen, for this would be arrogant. The Christian prays to get closer, to achieve understanding or in other words enlightenment, similar to the Buddhist. Any attempt to impose the will or cause chance is mere presumption. It is important to understand that truth comes in different 'languages', without changing the underlying meaning. In the place of *languages*, John Tavener talks of 'theophanies', in other words divine manifestations; *"God reveals Himself through his 'theophanies', whether it be through Christ, the Buddha, or virgin nature or in the word made book, The Koran. God shows himself in everything that lives and this includes the sublime language of music."* (44) Different religions belong to different cultures but all share a core belief system. For example, you might visit your local pub or bar because it is convenient and you wish to be sociable locally. You are not saying that it is the only pub in the world or that there are not others of equal worth. The Dalai Lama makes it crystal clear; *"humanity needs all the world's religions to suit the ways of life, diverse spiritual needs, and inherited national traditions of individual human beings."* And he goes further; *"every major religion of the world - Buddhism, Christianity, Confucianism, Hinduism, Islam, Jainism, Judaism, Sikhism, Taoism, Zoroastrianism - has similar ideals of love, the same goal of benefiting humanity through spiritual practice, and the same effect of making their followers into better human beings."* (45)

So with breathing and a clear open mind, we can achieve a state of awareness and balance that is wholly appropriate for sincere communication with others. Now sitting with that person, listening and concentrating on what they are trying to communicate will come naturally. To do this while giving your time will be appreciated as the great gift it is and may be sufficient without offering advice or a personal opinion. It will certainly give sufficient reward to oneself, as the pleasure that comes from pure giving. The expression of love is closely related to time, in as much as the application of love needs time, although of course they are not synonymous.

In the pure sense, The Prophet was right to say; *"you talk when you cease to be at peace with your thoughts."*(46) We have the notion of the 'strong silent type', as someone who doesn't need to chatter. The Prophet had a point because silence or listening is definitely a strength. In a social setting we can feel our own holding back as shyness or not participating but it is rarely perceived as this by others. This is a useful fact to bear in mind for the naturally reticent. In fact, to listen carefully and ask appropriate, perhaps penetrating questions is always perceived as impressive. So there is no need to pontificate on subjects upon which you feel you should be knowledgeable, when gleaning information from others is not only sufficient in itself but actually considered socially preferable. Far from exhibiting ignorance, it tends to make the listener appear attentive, considerate and interested and there is nothing more complimentary to others. It also puts them in control as the one directing the conversation; another apparent irony in a world in which nothing is quite as it appears.

It is worth considering an example of how this works in practice. Suppose for the sake of argument, that you have a close relative with whom you are having trouble relating. You perceive that they have ignored you, that they have shown little respect and perhaps don't seem to care as they should. This is likely to establish resentment in your mind, even though you want to be open and loving with them. You might hold back from communicating but if you did contact them, you are aware that the feelings you have might create an edge in your voice and barb what you say or even lead to inappropriate words and actions. You are right to hold back until you have taken the opportunity to reflect and consider the true nature of the situation. It might be worth consulting a trusted confidant, someone with an open and clear mind and a generous heart, who can offer a fresh perspective. Then it's over to you to search your mind or spirit, call it what you will and reflect, meditate or pray. It will inevitably begin to dawn that being ignored, disrespected or uncared-for are all likely to be your perceptions, your own feelings and possibly quite unrelated to that relative's perspective. It is possible their position will be different and that they in turn are quite unaware of your feelings.

As you continue in you reflective exercise, it will become apparent that you both approach things differently, that you may have overlooked various factors that make their behaviour understandable. There will be circumstances that you had forgotten or considerations overlooked. You will gain sympathy and empathy and hopefully the resentment will slip away, as your understanding increases. Now you can communicate with them with the confidence that you wish simply to spend time with them, enjoying their company and without any agenda in your mind. For in the end, even if there are issues that you perceive and even if you still feel you have been aggrieved, these are still your issues and no one else's. You can gently make others aware of your feelings but when it comes to their emotions and perceptions; *"you cannot burst the bubbles of others,"*(47) only our own. In the end it is none of our business.

Listening requires time and is most effective, when time is readily given to 'being' and not solely 'doing'. If you value the art of listening you will award it the time to work and this will be found to reap rich benefits. Another way of achieving the same goal is by slowing down every function that need not be undertaken at speed. Then one is naturally creating the opportunity for greater awareness, which of course then saves you time anyway; *"Modern man thinks he loses something - time - when he does not do things quickly; yet he does not know what to do with the time he gains - except kill it."*(48)

The 'strong silent type' knows that it is not what you do or say that counts but what you are and that will be little affected in people's perception by anything you say. This is a hard lesson to learn for many of us and we can waste a lot of time trying to appear to others in such a light, while being blissfully unaware of the subtle signs we are able to read in others. Much has been written about body language but a leap forward in the public conscience was achieved as a result of the writings of Desmond Morris in the 1970s.(49)

"Prayer is not an old woman's idle amusement.
Properly understood and applied, it is the most potent instrument
of action" (50)

STEP 4

CENTERING

"With realisation of one's own potential and self-confidence in one's ability, one can build a better world" (51)

It is important to be truly open to the world's challenges and what we have so far considered will strengthen us in that resolve. But almost as a counter-balance we will need to be properly grounded. So this step is about taking strength from constant, reliable truths as a platform from which to explore the world.

It is as well to be cautious of the debate between *nature* and *nurture*; cautious of seeing everything as black and white, as one or the other. Our world is more complex than we could ever imagine and the characteristics we develop in life should be seen as a cocktail of natural and nurtured influences. It is sobering to consider, as the geneticists would have us believe, that whatever one does in life, physically and mentally, the same unaltered genes are passed on to any offspring. This is to suggest that while we are affected by nurture in the world around us, our descendents are not as a result. This could be seen as proof of the futility of life's struggle or perhaps as a bit of a relief, when the slate of all one's feeble endeavours is eventually wiped clean.

What we can say with some certainty is that the so-called 'formative years' are far earlier than normally presumed. The most important years of influence are well before adolescence. In fact it is believed by many that the nurturing influence is at its greatest after birth and decreases exponentially until around the age of six, when outside influences become negligible. The emphasis placed on the importance of the adolescent years has arisen because this is when one comes under more sophisticated social influences. Though the reactive adolescent behaviour may be seen as a successfully staged 'teenage revolt', it is more likely evidence of involvement in the cementing of social habits. In other words, it represents a final bid for freedom in the face of overbearing and ultimately near unavoidable social pressures.

At some point well before adolescence, the child will become aware of the great dichotomy of life. This, the strange schizoid nature of adult psyche is probably 'tolerated' by the child until puberty, when it is then challenged for the illogical deception it is discovered to be. It is the coming to terms with this sham that dictates much of the 'fireworks' of adolescence and how it is resolved can determine degrees of success in life.

What is this dichotomy? It is the great chasm implicit in the phrase "*do what I say, not what I do*". Children's understanding is constantly underestimated in a modern society that has come to obsess on their innocence. Very early, children notice the gulf between adult words and deeds, even between the deeds and the spirit behind them. The young are told not to lie, deceive, lose their temper, be fearful or greedy and yet they will perceive these characteristics in adults and emulate them. For it is through the most basic of instincts to imitate, that the child learns the tricks for survival. For example, anger is so close to fear, that if the parent should become emotional explaining simple wrongdoing, the child will pick up that fear above all else. The lesson will be to fear what the parent obviously fears, while the parent's intended lesson is lost.

There may well be an element of this schizoid behaviour in all societies but it is all the more prevalent in our modern industrial age, where form and content have become disconnected. The dichotomy requires an agility of mind to bridge this so-called gap; the gap between what appears to be the case and what actually happens. It is possible that the development of schizophrenia is one type of coping mechanism in the face of a nurturing that appears incomprehensible. This would be evidence of that nature/nurture 'cocktail'. For some, different personas or even voices represent conflicting positions that appear otherwise insoluble to them. This need not be a pathological state, in fact to different degrees we are all required to departmentalise experiences and ideas in order to manage them. We cope with different methods and with differing degrees of success. It is important because a proper understanding of our imperfect world helps us to function within it. Finding the balance is crucial to feeling centred.

Freudian psychology highlighted the *gap* that opens up between a mother and child that must be resolved.(52) It is in effect part of the same *void* considered in Step 1, where the only appropriate *filler* is love. Unfortunately, confronted by the void

33

and the dichotomy, many struggle to come to terms with either and grow up confused, if not angry. There exists a real risk of finding methods to smother the apparent pain that this produces. The multitude of methods employed, range from conditions such as anorexia nervosa or chemical abuse, to over work and even suicide. Addictions can come in almost any form and should be classified as such as soon as we lose the power to control our cravings.

In the same way that nature and nurture are debated, the notion of *discipline* is the subject of much interpretation and misunderstanding. The ability to follow a predetermined path towards a recognised goal plays an important part in becoming centred because without it you will fail to nudge yourself into a balanced position. This is self-discipline and to a great extent relies on 'the tools you are given', in other words, the self-discipline of your parents and other role models. This essential discipline is a strength worth giving some consideration. It is a subtle power that if manifest in the parent through example alone, will be apparent and reassuring to the child. Then inherited by that child, it will forever be deemed as 'inner strength' and of lasting value throughout life. It is the power to avoid unnecessary conflicts and without it, life will be far more of a struggle and the risk of addiction much greater. But in recognising this powerful influence as the greatest gift possible to any child, we should not forget the additional and unavoidable requirement for personal application in any decision. This is 'free will' and to ignore its existence is to abrogate responsibility, either from oneself or from sections of society demeaned by the assumption of incapacity.

We should perhaps remind ourselves here that power comes in different guises. There is of course the power of military might, of brute strength and political power as exercised within a democratic state. There is the familiar power of money, a form of energy in its own right. But then more subtly, there is the power of influence, coming from respect or fear. As examples, the Queen of England or the Pope hold this power and use it subliminally to different degrees. Particularly because it is not so obvious and specifically because it is intangible, this power is often underestimated. Being truly centred is about recognising how to influence others from a position of inner strength.

The need for careful balancing and discipline becomes apparent when one considers the dangers of power, and it is unquestionably very dangerous. Without doubt we are all susceptible to the intoxication of power to varying degrees where democrats become 'inebriated' and the dictators full-blown 'alcoholics'. Unless we acknowledge this fact, we are apt to class everyone as either good or evil, providing another example of the triumph of the simplistic over the simple. To do so is to risk failing to identify the causes of corruption in human nature and therefore to be dangerously vulnerable to it. When power corrupts, nuance is lost. Unpalatable as it may seem, the democratically elected Adolf Hitler was as human as the rest of us.

The empowering effects of being centred are familiar to anyone trained in a specific sporting discipline, such as the martial arts. For example, there is a popular preconception that a heavyweight boxer will dominate, if ever pitted against a Thai boxer half his weight. But those familiar with these relative sports will know better. The Thai boxer, as in all the martial arts, holds back, constrains, centres and then projects with lightening speed. Several mental or 'spiritual' qualities come together to his advantage but it is his smaller size that will give him the physical edge for concentrated acceleration. That speed is a physical advantage to balance the advantage of mass, is appreciated by the science of Isaac Newton and the application of Bruce Lee,(53) but it is the 'spirit'; the centeredness that gives our Thai boxer the capacity to prevail.

This popular misconception is also an understandable result of the modern obsession with size. Whereas in reality, as soon as size outgrows the limitations of human scale, cohesion is lost; *"Man is small, and, therefore, small is beautiful."*(54) Size matters if you are a stag surviving in the wilds but not to social humans. Yet the club wielding mentality of many modern males is a parody of any reality in nature. The gentle demeanour observed in males cut off from modern civilisation and when at rest, is perhaps testament to this. It is not that they do not become aggressive but that traditionally, anger required a real crisis, rather than the constant 'rage' manufactured by the modern predicament.

It appears that in post-industrial societies, as the real need for hot-blooded males has receded, there has developed an inverse macho culture to compensate. Men deny their true selves by denying their more feminine tendencies. As if that were not enough, many women, in a desire to enjoy what they assumed to be the superior attributes of the male, have done exactly the opposite. Too many have become just as much the parody of their true natures. The irony is that macho men end up enfeebled 'boys' without the balance and inner strength to centre them. While women, abhorring the weakness in men, have often stepped into the breach and assumed an aberrant power, which by its brutal execution has left them diminished and confused. Men and women need each other because they each bring the complementary forces of the generally less passionate judgment of one and the less conditional *compassion* of the other. Robbed of the spirit of pure compassion, humanity is chronically disabled. The natural attributes of women - to nurture and love unconditionally - are as important to the equation as any male attribute, without which the balance is lost and true centeredness is impossible.

It is vital that both sexes rediscover their uniqueness and individual strengths, so that they can live equally with their many similarities. When they do this, they encompass naturally many of the characteristics of the opposite sex without need for any pretension. This is a liberating realisation and can only result in healthier interaction between the sexes. It is healthier to break down the barriers that have developed between male and female and equally between old and young. Then it is possible to be able to relate to all people not as different ages or sexes but as warm, individual human beings. It becomes possible to enjoy the company of people on many different levels. Ignoring the existence of age and gender might suggest an entirely non-sexually aware friendship but any relationship can blossom into a state of healthy flirtation. It is perhaps wise here to clarify the intended meaning for this 'flirt'. To flirt here, is to give attention to, acknowledge the merit and enjoy the company of anyone. Ignoring age, for example, we can by our very application to another human being, acknowledge their life force, their inner (or maybe outer) beauty and rejoice in it. If genuine, it is hard to imagine anything more flattering or more empowering and it is a natural product of being truly centred.

There is a powerful truth here worth keeping in our minds. That if we are in the right place ourselves, it is quite impossible for those who interact with us to remain in the same position themselves. In any relationship, be it personal, family, friend or work, if we show our inner strength and stand firm in what we believe, then we can effect change. This is a natural extension to the call to listen because it proves that 'doing nothing' - an interesting oxymoron in itself - can be the most powerful act conceivable. This realisation might well be easier to implement within the work environment or even among friends. But it is much harder closer to home, within one's own family. Families represent a complex web of interrelationships, rivalries and understandings and are therefore able to test the strongest resolve; *"Only in his home town, among his relatives and in his own house is a prophet without honour"*.(55) Ancient wisdom endorses this truth and therefore real centred-ness is essential, if one is to be truly effective.

"So patiently persevere: for verily the promise of Allah is true: nor let those shake thy firmness, who have (themselves) no certainty of faith"(56)

STEP 5

HEALING

"In Tibet we say that many illnesses can be cured by the one medicine of love and compassion."(57)

You could say that while so far we have been laying foundations, now we can safely build a useful structure. Or as a tree with a sound network of roots below, we can enjoy the fruits above. We now have a solid framework of disciplined understanding that will allow our thinking to direct us more wisely.

The writer of 'The Road Less Travelled', M Scott-Peck, believed that Freudian perceptions might have placed too much emphasis on the subconscious mind and not enough on everyday thought. In his work as a psychiatrist, Scott-Peck was constantly confronted by patients with what he considered flawed thinking.(58) For a variety of reasons he witnessed a very conscious lack of clear reasoning that made life difficult and often led to psychiatric conditions. But he stressed this as coming from a conscious, rather than subconscious level and therefore possible to tackle directly and with reason. The Buddha put it another way,

"Every human being is the author of his own health or disease."(59) So this must give us hope, that at any stage in our life, we have the potential to change our thinking and improve our lives. If our personalities really are fixed, we must learn to live with them and know their flaws. But by contrast, our thinking we can work on and constantly improve. This in part is about recognising and living comfortably with one's own flaws and is sometimes termed as working; *". . . with our neurosis."*(60)

Clear thinking fosters peace of mind or ease of mind. A lack of this ease or 'dis-ease' if you like, is the wake created by fears, frustrations and hate, just as healing is the path left by love. It is important that we recognise the connectivity of these elements, where so often society unnaturally separates them. An example of this might be the inability to understand the possible link between a headache and being in a state of inner turmoil. In a society that values saleable commodities, the route cause is less useful than a marketable 'cure', forgetting, as we have seen, that headaches are not caused by a lack of painkillers.

So health and healing are as closely linked to love, as fear and frustration are to hate. We cannot therefore appreciate the nature of healing, health and love, without at the same time understanding the connections between fear, frustration and hate. With a clear understanding of the power of love, we can and should all become healers. If, as is commonly held, fear is usually the result of ignorance, while frustration is attempting what is unachievable, then it follows that hate, born of fear and frustration, must itself ripple out in the wake of ignorance and misunderstanding. The only cure is love and its healing power promotes ease of mind and body; *"Man should forget his anger before he lies down to sleep."*(61)

It is important to speak of the mind and body as one, for it has been the defining mistake of Western thinking and particularly of *'allopathic'* medicine (62) to separate the two. This separation grew in part out of the writings of Descartes who saw the mind and body as quite separate and the latter as a machine.(63) The problem was then compounded by the 'miraculous' discovery of Penicillin. While acknowledging its lifesaving practical application, it has undoubtedly inspired too great a dependence on cures in a bottle and distorted our appreciation of the oneness of the mind and body. Not only did this thinking deny the interdependence of mind and body, it inhibited both from allowing health to prevail. And it is after all, only an *'appreciation'* that we have, for *'understanding'* would be too strong a word to describe something still quite obviously beyond our full comprehension. It follows that if we do not recognise the limits of our understanding, we are at risk of distorting the truth and escalating our ignorance. Better to account for our inabilities to grasp the very complex natures of our bodies and avoid the past mistake of simplifying the body into separate units. While we should be aware of the steady progress being made by conventional Western medicine to adopt a more integrated, holistic approach, there still exists widespread ignorance. Specialist consultants can be the least enlightened here, still obsessed with cures for symptoms in body-parts and failing to treat the whole person. By inference, a well-informed, observant general practitioner has a far better opportunity to look beyond the surface and see the 'wood for the trees'.

That's probably quite enough fairly abstract theory and we should try to consider some practical applications. For example, imagine you are suffering stomach pains and flatulence, especially when you are hungry. A western allopathic doctor might say that you were suffering excess acidity in the stomach, possibly resulting in an ulcer, which might require a surgical operation. His diagnosis is a logical one based on the traditions of empirical evidence. But that necessarily also makes it a purely material one with - fortunately for the vast medical industry - material remedies both chemical and possibly surgical. But suppose you went to Africa to consult a traditional healer or 'nyanga'. He might suggest your problem was the result of the spirits of your ancestors. While at first this might seem farfetched to *Western thinking,*(64) we are all aware of the impact of our families and their fears and prejudices on our psyche, usually called the *superego*. While both approaches have a grasp of the truth, it could be argued the African doctor is nearer the cause and therefore the cure. The so-called witch doctor is of course alluding to the effect our minds and brains - nurtured by our backgrounds and family - can have on our bodies. This is a subtle relationship overlooked by the Cartesian tradition (65) that in crude terms, attempts to know all by compartmentalising what can only be cut up with a scalpel when already dead. Or in the words of the Erich Fromm; *"Western science . . . seeks the truth by means of dismembering life."*

Then consider the common cold. Have you ever wondered why these seem invariably to strike around holidays? While the effects of the cold appear to be activated solely by a virus, there are likely to be other factors that render the cause more complex. Our lives involve the inevitable absorption of a vast cocktail of toxins, from the air, in food and in many other forms. These must be eliminated somehow and during our lives of constraint and control, this release can often be inhibited, where constipation is an example of this. After perhaps a period of concentrated work and business before a break, the thought of relaxation alone can trigger what is in effect an unnatural release of toxins and the effects are felt in the common cold, as well as more serious conditions. Evidence of this can be experienced while engaging in a detoxifying regime of some kind. The effects seem to mimic the typical symptoms of a cold, including a sore throat or headache. A healthy body will eliminate constantly and reduce the likelihood of a cold developing. It is therefore important to respect the common cold for what it is and not attempting to stifle it, unless absolutely necessary.

Then consider the term *psychosomatic*. It is intended to express the obviously complex relationship between thought and effect. Western thinking is slowly coming to terms with this unavoidable relationship and its implications for generations who ignored it. We have witnessed the apparent mystery of the *placebo* effect. This 'mystery' is the equally unavoidable fact that medical conditions can often improve with the application of fake cures, usually in the form of a pill. There is obviously something going on in the human psyche that allows self-cure, when our minds choose it.

We should see this as an indication of much more to be understood than meets the eye of empirical research. There is a traditional response to the notion of the psychosomatic that suggests a sufferer has brought it on themselves, is merely *'making it up'* as *'it's all in the mind'*. The poverty of this kind of thinking betrays the very disconnection between mind and body. These disconnections arguably occur most during times in history of acute trauma such as war, when it is felt necessary to deny feelings and act purely out of compulsion or necessity. In reality, the word *psychosomatic,*(66) stems from our attempt to bridge this gap in our understanding and reconnect once again. It alludes to the effects that mental conditions can have on the body but also those that the body can have on our mentality. It is well know that in certain conditions, one affecting the other, continuously over a debilitating period, can cause a downward spiral in health.

Another clue into this complex union of mind and body is in how and what we eat. We are aware of the importance of healthy foods. As a guide, these are natural foods, foods that we have been adapted to eat for thousands of years. The elements making up these foods come in recognisable proportions and when you change these relative quantities, the body will struggle to cope. Two simple examples of this are salt and sugar. While they are substances that occur naturally, they are not in the concentrations found in modern foods. These unnatural concentrations create an imbalance, which can trigger short-term problems such heart disease and obesity. But they can also risk long-term, life-threatening conditions such as cancer. The reasons for the development of these various concentrations in our diets are complex and in our mind-set. But while the cravings are both physical and financial, they are not the subject of this book. Our interest here is not so much in the effect of *what* you eat, as *how* you eat. It is some indication of the power of the mind and its close interaction with the body, that your mentality or changing mood has a crucial effect on diet and absorption. We have previously touched on the *sympathetic* and *parasympathetic* modes.(67) They show for example, that if you attempt to eat when the mind/body is in fight or flight mode - and this can simply be a stressful day at work - then absorption will be greatly compromised. And in this we see another indication of that subtle relationship in action.

The examples above show the dangers of attempting to interrupt the natural and healthy relationship between mind and body. This is the relationship between the immaterial and the material, though the description of them as distinct entities is itself unhelpful. The language isn't a great deal of help here. Notice how we describe anything non-material, which is spiritual as *immaterial*, suggesting of no consequence.(68) It should of course be more accurately defined as of no immediate obvious consequences, which is a very different matter. This misunderstanding causes many of the medical problems that confront us today and to *heal* is to appreciate and work with this relationship. If you take medication when it is not necessary, you confuse the complex body system and by inference yourself. But equally damagingly, there are many medications that can positively harm the system. An obvious example of this is antibiotics. While they can eradicate harmful bacteria, they can also destroy the body's natural immune system and the long-term effects can be serious debilitation.

We have touched on the notion of healing but not specifically how to heal. We have considered some of the elements of the mind/body relationship and that one cannot consider one without the other. It is undeniable that physical symptoms can be improved by material means. For example, we recognise the logic of *"feed a cold, starve a fever"*. But we have seen that *how* you eat is as important as *what* you eat. The correct mental state is just as

45

important in regaining and maintaining health as any pill or surgery. It therefore follows that a positive mentality will as much maintain and improve health, as a negative one will debilitate it. We need to be clear what promotes ease and wellbeing in the mind, so that we can tap into the force that heals.

One of the tragedies of *Cartesian Dualism* was the confusion it caused in the area of sensuality. We have come to see *love* and *sex* as separate acts, where so often the former - as an abstract mental state - is considered positive and the latter - as a 'base' desire - as negative; one as selfless and the other selfish. But there is no logic behind this, just a territorial possessiveness built on fear. Even the word sex, has come to imply simply the act of penetration and there is no word to describe any of a large range of other sensual, 'social' activities possible between humans. The unfortunate result has been that any physical contact - and despite the insinuation our language carries, this includes just touching - is considered a violation and to be mistrusted, if not actually litigated against.

Unfortunately, state religions have hardly helped here. The requirement to cover the body and abstain from physical contact has lead to a widespread culture of guilt around any physical expression of genuine love. A church that forbids contraception in order to preserve the sanctity of life, while supporting war and the death penalty is clearly contradicting itself. The issue here is one of domination and control; in the words of Erich Fromm; *"the breaking of human will is the reason for vilifying sex."* However, nature gives us a range of activities from body language and touch to massage that are expressions of trust, bonding and giving. None need be inappropriate or pose a threat to integrity but all can possess the healing force, where touch can be argued to be vital to human health.

What is this healing force? The answer is both complex and wonderfully simple. By any method of application, love is the only cure. But even with a language as rich as English, there are nuances of understanding difficult to articulate easily. We now have an indication of what we mean by healing but what do we mean by love? Let us consider the nature of love, to understand that it is more than related to healing, it is actually symbiotic with it. It is perhaps easier to immediately consider what love is not. In an age when almost everything else can be said to be a commodity, love is not one. This is important because it is constantly and unhelpfully treated as such. With a commodity, you can buy it, you can store it and you can sell it. It's true, you could also give it away but then you would still have lost that commodity, in other words you'd be the poorer for it. Love is different and the only other obvious force to compare is the energy of the sun, to which it may well be related. The sun's rays fall on all of us alike and are unconditional. Love cannot be a commodity because the more you give, the more you have to give. 'Expenditure' of love makes your 'stock' grow rather than diminish. In reality, to talk of love as a commodity is obviously pointless. But we need to be aware of the difference to understand how we should deal with love.

Love also does not reside in any object. It may have had a relationship with something material, as a kiss might be related to an act of loving but it will not reside in the material. This is an important distinction, for we all too easily grasp the material as manifestations of love, when love itself has swiftly moved on. The monotheistic religions are conscious of the risks of worshiping the material, even if they have not always lead by example and Jesus made it the foundation of his teaching. In fact, it is possible that the kiss of Judas was intended as a metaphor to prove conclusively that love resides in nothing physical.(69)

For love is not tangible but a spirit and as such it is constant and it is boundless *"the vessel that gives forever."*(70) Shakespeare beautifully described this in the words; *"My bounty is as boundless as the sea, my love as deep. The more I give to thee the more I have, for both are infinite."*(71) However, love must not be confused with charity, which is of course a 'cold' commodity. So what *is* love and how do we recognise it? We know it is a spirit and we know it is boundless, which in itself may prove seeking an exact definition as impossible. But that said, it does have other recognisable characteristics. It is selfless, it has total faith and as mentioned before, it is the source of all health. That's probably as close a definition as we'll reach but we should attempt to define what we mean exactly by *faith* and *health*.

As previously mentioned, by faith, we're not talking about any particular religion, with a capital F or specific creed. Our interest is with faith itself; faith in life; faith that the sky will not fall on your head; that strangers in the street will not attack you; that you are loved; that the sun will rise tomorrow and that there is hope and meaning in the world. With this belief one has faith and this is crucially linked to the boundless energy that is love. Without it, loving would be unsustainable. This is why you must *"love like you've never been hurt."*(72) The alternative is to lose faith, which is to lose everything that matters.

And by health, we are talking about peace of mind through love, love that is the "bread of life", the very thing that sustains us and brings us ease, the profound ease that avoids 'dis-ease'. The implication of this is enormous. For it is likely that the greatest ingredient in any cure, in any act that brings people to a happier, more comfortable position, will be the application of love. So it matters little whether you administer a placebo; a herbal poultice; needles through the skin; gentle massage; waving watches or just sit with them in silence, if you are giving of your time and obviously caring deeply, you will be curing and restoring. Call it a miracle if you like, because it is and may always be, beyond understanding but you will be giving the life-force and what we all crave to exist and thrive. The proof of its power will be the simple fact that by giving you will feel yourself empowered and restored yourself. This may come as a real surprise but it should be taken as proof enough that you are dealing with something beyond a commodity - if you like, handling the light of the sun.(73) This is 'compassion' and for definitive proof, we could turn again to the understanding of the Dalai Lama; "*A mind committed to compassion is like an overflowing reservoir - a constant source of energy, determination and kindness . . . The compassionate mind is like an elixir; it is capable of transforming bad situation into beneficial ones. Therefore, we should not limit our expressions of love and compassion to our family and friends. Nor is the compassion only the responsibility of clergy, health care and social workers. It is the necessary business of every part of the human community*". (74)

In summary, to heal is to give of the primordial force of life. If the Buddha was right and we are all the authors of our own health and disease, then we should consider M Scott-Peck's call to right thinking. If we are thinking straight, our minds will be at ease and that will affect our bodies and we will naturally affect those around us too. Mental health is sometimes measured in the same respect as physical fitness. During cardio-vascular testing for fitness, the heart rate is less important than the time it takes for it to return to its normal rate. You can likewise undertake this test for the health of your own mentality. We all get angry or low at times but the indicator of health is how quickly you can return to a state of honest composure.

There is a useful exercise to help start this process and place the mind in the right state. Take an opportunity to consider the positive in your life. Perhaps before going to sleep, you may be able to contemplate some of the following: I am without pain, I am healthy, my body is clean, my sheets soft, my bed comfortable, my room orderly, my roof sound, my house intact and secure, my partner loving, my family and friends constant, my country at peace. Tomorrow the sun may shine and I will have food to eat, hopes fulfilled and the opportunity to change the world a little for the better. If you can boast most of these things, then you are truly rich, rich in faith and love.

"All that we are is the result of what we have thought.
If a man speaks or acts with an evil thought, pain follows him.
If a man speaks or acts with a pure thought, happiness follows
him, like a shadow that never leaves him" (75)

STEP 6

RESPECTING

*"I am a Muslim and a Hindu and a Christian
and a Jew and so are all of you"* (76)

Ascending Step 5 will release a powerful creative force within us, a force capable of no less than healing the world around us. We have seen how this is both beneficial to others and to ourselves. Also, how benefiting personally might come as a surprise, having committed in a spirit of altruism. However, the awareness of that personal gain should be considered proof enough of its validity. This is because the relationship needs to always be reciprocal or the sole beneficiary would feel indebted by your 'benevolence' and the love would turn to 'cold charity'. It would hardly be an act of generosity that left others feeling less by comparison. Even more dangerous is the risk that through our generosity to others we should feel worthier than them. With this attitude Step 6 would be impossible to achieve successfully, as respect would be difficult.

You will have heard it said that respect must be earned. On the face of it, this might sound reasonable enough but why? Why should we have to prove ourselves worthy? Surely you would only need to do this to someone lacking faith or confidence, someone who was fearful of those around them. Step 5 has shown us that the mature attitude is to have faith and trust. To do otherwise is to invite mistrust from others. The strength here is in being able to set the 'gold standard' regardless of the circumstances, for others to recognise and follow. By becoming an 'actor' rather than 'reactor', one is placing an essential foundation stone for a civil society.

Surely, if we are enlightened we give of our trust, our love, freely and without prejudice. We prove our maturity by confidence in others and it is well known that where faith is given, faith will be returned. Of course there is a risk that the trust will be abused but that is no reason not to give it in the first place. In fact, it is the very risk one takes in showing that faith and trust that gives it such power and makes it so effective. This is the true meaning of respect and when given without condition, is a good definition of civilisation.

It is easy to like those close to us. Respect for familiar friends and family is not difficult. Honouring those who are different is the requirement here, made plain by Jesus in his teachings; ". . *Love your enemies, bless them that curse you . . "*(77) And here we come up against what appears a basic human characteristic; the tribal, herding instinct that distinguishes between friend and foe. But however natural it may seem, it is irrelevant to the developed, mature human of the 21st century. For one thing, even the most primitive of humans can extend the 'herd' without effort. We know this can include vast numbers, whole nations or even greater ethnic groups. Why shouldn't humans recognise all humans as of the same genus and without much effort, achieve amity?

Animosity relies on fear and ignorance. It is surely our duty to strive constantly towards understanding what is different between humans; or when that is not possible, to accept the distinction as valid and live respectfully with it. There is a saying, *"to know a man you must know his history."*(78) We're not going to expel that fear or ignorance without some effort. But the reward is understanding and tolerance as we get to know individuals and cultures. Understanding will inevitably reveal by comparison to oneself, both the less fortunate in certain areas and the more gifted in others and that helps develop a balanced perspective.

In the end surely respect is about not judging others and accepting them as they are. Gossip is invariably about judging both people's actions and also their motives. Judging motives is always dangerous because however healthy they may appear, how can we ever really know another's motivation? But we live in a world where motives are constantly assumed and without that assumption being contested. Queen Elizabeth I was considered wise in part because she understood this dictum well and is remembered for saying that she had; *"no desire to make windows into men's souls."*(79) In other words, she didn't need or have the right to know what was going on deep inside the mind of others, just that they act according to the law. Central to an understanding of respect is a respect for the privacy of others.

And maybe that is at the heart of the spirit of respect. Respect for the individual's independence allows us to give respect on many levels. We can respect those we consider less fortunate than ourselves; those less able, with all their imperfections. This allows us to respect the natural world in all its guises. Consider the harmless spider living in your home. In ignorance you might be scared of what you do not know and that would translate into aggression or cruelty. But appreciating its part to play, its equal right to exist and for 'privacy', one could respect that spider and if necessary, care for it. Your role would change from a victim of the world to one of its benefactors, with higher responsibility but also greater rewards.

Knowledge will inform us that we are as imperfect as anything or anyone else. Part of tolerance is appreciating that what we see as imperfection in others, is actually part of a rich tapestry of characteristics that make people what they are. Very often, to tamper with the characteristics of others, is to attempt to pick and choose from something that is rightfully a whole. Respect is acknowledging the rights of others to be different and be prepared to live with it.

For example, black and white are arbitrary distinctions, without real significance. Some humans are darker than others, while some have physical characteristics that get them labelled 'black'. Ill informed history has created a racial myth, that ignores the equal success that knowledge informs us is the reality of 'black' characteristics. One could illustrate this by considering at this moment, the most respected politician; Nelson Mandela or the fastest human; Usain Bolt, the most esteemed preacher; Martin Luther King, the highest paid media personality; Oprah Winfrey, the "most powerful man in the world"; Barak Obama and one could go on. This is not to distinguish one random group from another, for to do so would be to fall into that same racist trap. No, the intention is simply to show the meaninglessness of prejudice and in this example, the insignificance of colour.

So we respect those we might otherwise have demeaned but should not we also extend equal respect to those we consider better qualified? Without a healthy respect for authority what hope is there for any social system? Because we didn't set it up ourselves, a system is necessarily no less valid or worthy. It would follow then, that anything we were loosely involved in, such as a government set up through the admittedly imperfect system we call democracy, we really do have an obligation to value and support. Otherwise it could be argued, we are guilty of double standards. If you choose to remain in a society, you are surely under some obligation to respect its systems and work within them towards any desired change. It is an argument sometimes made by those disapproving of industrial action. They would maintain that by entering upon a contract with a business employer, the employee owes some loyalty and respect. While this position may itself not respect the hard won democratic right for fairness in the workplace, there is definitely a balance to be considered.

It is partly through greater freedom of information and communication that societies have come under greater scrutiny. This in turn has revealed greater corruption, in once respected figureheads and institutions. If some imperfection is an unavoidable fact of life, there is a risk of denying all respect under the unvarying assumption of corruption. It would appear that by this simplistic logic, we have seen a breakdown in respect for all institutions, including governments, titular heads and spiritual leaders. With the same brush we have also swept away respect for such traditional role models as parents and teachers. In ancient Greece, the teacher was respected above all others and with good reason. What greater role could society give than to trust its future to those preparing and inspiring? And to this great task society entrusted those, not with specialist knowledge in one subject but with inner strength, care and experience in life. The aim being not so much to train in any one discipline but to enthuse through example and leave the student hungry for knowledge and personal improvement. As has been seen, these are of course the very same qualities required of parents. Far Eastern cultures in particular, have shown by tradition, a greater respect for parents and forefathers.

Of course, to a great extent respect for figures of authority has been lost for understandable reasons. Teachers, like many other possible role models have come under the corrosive influence of a sick society. A society that values the tangible above all else, will struggle to recognise and value a *spiritual* teacher. For any teacher who inspires and fosters personal growth and true freedom of thought will come under huge pressure to meet the expectations of the day. Again, Erich Fromm had the words to articulate this problem; *"Today, millions of people in America and Europe try to find contact with tradition and with teachers that can show them the way. But in large part the doctrines and teachers are either fraudulent or vitiated by the spirit of public relations ballyhoo, or mixed up with the financial or prestige interests of the respective gurus."*(80)

Knowledge informs us that the world is complex and full of nuance. Our modern-day thirst for information has not always been matched by depth of understanding. The curse of the modern sound-bite culture means few actually bother to pursue any one issue to a satisfactory conclusion. Ignorance is only blissful when *"a little knowledge is a dangerous thing."*(81) It is just too easy to dismiss what we do not understand or would rather belittle. We may never understand the complexities of the human brain. Even without really knowing how much of our brains we use, we do now appreciate that it is deeply complex and works on many levels. The terms 'bright', 'stupid' or 'brainy' just don't seem to mean much, when there is so broad a function range. For example, there is the facility to manage numbers, remember facts and process information quickly. But there is also the ability to judge distances, coordinate brain and body or reason in depth. Greater understanding of this apparently unfathomable organ must lead to greater respect for nature but also for the different gifts that a brain can provide different people.

Despite the modern emphasis on the accumulation of knowledge, it is not actually the information itself that makes us respected by others. What really matters is the drive; the desire to understand and the spirit of conciliation that leads us to explore, to grow spiritually and mature. An indication of our confusion about this matter is evident from how 'stupid' many very 'clever' people can appear. It can be baffling to witness and we tend to put them down as having little common sense. But why should someone with great skills with numbers or remembering information, be wise or perceptive? Again, rich as our languages are, they cannot articulate these matters clearly and this therefore inhibits our understanding. We are thrown back on the much-maligned word 'spirit' to convey this positive attitude.

Professor Richard Dawkins describes this positive spirit as the *"Theory of Altruism."*(82) He sees it as a vestige of a primitive respect for our particular family or group, from a distant time when it had to be defended. But while the origins of this emotion are not and may never be fully understood, it is surely only practical to embrace it and extend it to cover all life on this planet. There is no logic against it and every reason to promote it. Why need we be slaves to our past (or present) and merely accept our 'biological' forms as the constraint with which we are lumbered? We need here imagination, inspiration or faith, call it what you will to drive us to greater understanding. Then *". . . you will know the truth, and the truth will set you free."*(83)

That said, we should bear in mind one great caveat. While all the above leads one to judge with compassion and care, there are different definitions to the word 'judge'. A court judges those that break the law and as individuals we judge situations. We have no need to judge other individuals or groups. The great religions of the world agree that the existence of genuine humility eliminates the need. If we have no ego feeding off our vulnerabilities, we feel no need to judge others and then respect comes naturally and from the heart. In the words of the Hindu monk Kaliyaphani; *"In the Eastern viewpoint, this body is not who we are; we are the soul that animates it. When you 'see' that soul, you have tremendous respect for the equality and rights of every tiny creature and you don't have to get caught up in judging anyone. It's a very liberating feeling."*(84)

*". . . In order to arrive at what you do not know,
You must go by a way which is the way of ignorance"*(85)

STEP 7

FORGIVING

*"An eye for an eye only ends up
making the whole world blind"*(86)

Step 7 is certainly a challenge for many but having climbed the steps below, we are in better shape to take it in our stride. From here on, the view will improve and we will see with greater clarity and logic and this growing enlightenment will give us greater purpose.

Forgiveness should be honoured as an all-powerful force for good. After all, it is accepted as a structural tenet of all the major world religions, though they may debate and contrast the varying weight placed upon it. There is always the risk of muddying the water with interminable semantics and interpretations as each religious discipline is subject to contracting language, historic distinction and sectarian division. Only a fool would attempt to make definitive statements on the subject on behalf of the different 'Faiths'. That said, any student of comparative religion would confirm the huge significance of forgiving across the divides.

Let us simply consider the monotheistic religions. The Old Testament scriptures speak for them all; *"Come now, let us reason together,"* says the Lord. *"Though your sins are like scarlet, they shall be as white as snow; though they are red as crimson, they shall be like wool." "For I desire mercy, not sacrifice, and acknowledgment of God rather than burnt offerings."*(87) In Islam the Koran identifies God as; *"the Most Gracious, the Most Merciful, and the Most Beneficent"* and more merciful to His creatures than a mother to her child.(88) C. Mueen-Uddin, a founder of the Muslim Council of Britain, is in no doubt that Islam places mercy and forgiveness at its heart; *"Islam gives hope to mankind. There are many narrations that display the quality and attribute of Allah's mercy. Indeed, He is 'ar-Rahman', the Most Compassionate, and 'ar-Raheem', the Most Merciful. Allah tells man of the greatness of His forgiveness and mercy so that no one would despair due to the amount of sins he may have committed."*(89)

In Judaism Yom Kippur is known as the Day of Atonement; *". . . We are first to acknowledge our 'sins' against others, and then make reparations. In turn, we ask for forgiveness and it is expected that just as each of us hopes that others will forgive us, we are expected to forgive others for their sins against us."*(90) Christians sometimes assume that in Judaism, the requirement is entirely on the perpetrator to seek forgiveness from the wronged but there is no evidence of this; *"It is forbidden to be obdurate and not allow yourself to be appeased. On the contrary, one should be easily pacified and find it difficult to become angry. When asked by an offender for forgiveness, one should forgive with a sincere mind and a willing spirit . . . forgiveness is natural to the seed of Israel."*(91)

No religion could claim to put the notion of forgiveness more squarely at the core of its creed than Christianity and Jesus spoke continuously of its importance. The 'Parable of the Prodigal Son'(92) together with the 'Parable of the unforgiving servant'(93) are perhaps the best known references. But also in his most significant teaching episode at the Sermon on the Mount, Jesus made forgiveness the heart of his massage; *"Blessed are the merciful, for they will be shown mercy."*(94) ; *"If someone strikes you on one cheek, turn to him the other also."*(95) ; *"Be merciful, just as your Father is merciful."*(96) ; *"Do not judge, and you will not be judged. Do not condemn, and you will not be condemned. Forgive, and you will be forgiven."*(97) These are quotes from the New Testament and it is not always understood, even by Christians, that it represents a new approach or 'Covenant', which though building on the old, by definition, superseded it. Any notion of revenge, as in an *"eye for an eye, a tooth for a tooth,"*(98) was to be left behind for good. Perhaps in requiring a new Covenant, the Bible was itself recognising that humans had evolved and required different standards. In this context the *Theory of Altruism,*(99) with its attempt to understand us as both kind hearted and primordial, itself begins to look a little archaic.

But in interpreting Darwin so that we view ourselves as victims of our own *'Selfish'* genes, we limit in our minds the ability to escape our immediate, self-centred needs. Worse still, we condemn ourselves to a form of hell on earth, where we are all assumed to live by a base common denominator from which we cannot advance. It is as dangerous to assume we live in a world of purely selfish acts, as it is to ignore the cruelty of injustice around us. But love and forgiveness appear as natural to us as any selfish act and there is plenty of evidence to prove that forgetting forgiveness actually depresses us. In fact, even if Jews can forget it, Judaism recognises this today more than ever; *"In Western society, aversion to apology is a widespread malady. Whether somebody cuts another off in traffic, or destroys a marriage, admitting guilt is out of vogue. In fact, pop psychology has done all it can to remove the whole concept of 'guilt' from our lexicon. It's much easier to rationalise our mistakes away. And it's unhealthy to feel guilt, they say. 'Suppress it!' On one level, this suppression is unhealthy. When we refuse to admit, it is depressing and paralysing. The regret stays inside and festers."*(100)

This statement by a well respected rabbi, recognises that the act of forgiving others, frees us from our own anger and resentment. Failing to forgive will no doubt hurt the wrongdoer but it will cause as much or more harm to us in not being able to forgive. We can say therefore, that it is generally accepted as the obligation of whoever wrongs us to seek forgiveness from us and with a *contrite heart*.(101) This act, the act of contrition or remorse is important for the wrongdoer's own long-term benefit through peace of mind. But it should in the end be of little consequence to us for we are all individuals, with sole responsibility for our destinies. When the contrition of others becomes important to us, then we are missing the point. And it is an important point, because without moving beyond an unhealthy attachment to whoever confronts us, we will struggle to climb the next two steps. Resolution and good leadership will be hard to achieve while we cling to personal resentments. These resentments can easily find focus on others who we see harming us but in the end, they come from our inner self and must be confronted.

As much as anything, this is an issue of discernment and judgment in any situation. Logically, we will find it harder to forgive others, where we have judged them to be wrong and lesser than us for it. Similarly, it is much easier to forgive those with whom you can truly empathise. We can see here the obvious risk of prejudice and therefore the logical necessity to avoiding judging others altogether; "*Judge not, that ye be not judged.*"(102) If we don't judge we can relate to others on a level playing field and thereby free our own minds because of it.

That said, we do need to remember that distinction we made in the word *judgment*. We all need to judge situations and everyone with whom we interact, to assess their purpose and intentions. But this is distinct from being judgmental or if you like, condemning them with our judgment. Besides, as we have already observed, it is hard if not impossible to really know the mind of others, let alone their intentions. Tavener's logic is easy to follow; "*The Roman Church will tell you, if you do this you'll go there, if you do that you'll go someplace else. It feels as if you're arriving at Heathrow Airport. But we don't know the judgment of God - no-one knows*".(103) It is again an issue of privacy and by observing the right of others to it, we help ourselves. Mother Teresa put it simply; "*If you judge people, you have no time to love them.*"(104) *For-giving* then becomes a gift of love, given without thought of return. This is because a gift with a 'return' of any kind is not a gift at all, it is a deal and therefore merely an exchange of goods or commodities. Giving or forgiving is its own reward and it really is true that "*what goes around comes around.*"(105)

So we have seen forgiveness accepted throughout history as vital to healthy human relations. We have seen that by forgiving, we give solace and relief to others but also to ourselves. It is a powerfully proactive move that comes from a position of understanding and strength and is therefore a part of loving and healing. In the words of Mohandas Gandhi; *"The weak can never forgive. Forgiveness is the attribute of the strong."*(106)

We will know when this step is truly climbed, for judgement itself will eventually become an irrelevant issue. This is because modesty, humility and compassion will make forgiveness unnecessary, for we will appreciate that there is nothing to forgive. This sentiment and the risks of judging others is echoed in the words; *"Many by me their judge when I had breath, were to confinement sent to meet their death. Now breathless I without the strength to budge, lie here confined by death to meet my judge."* However it is most clearly articulated in the Hindu scriptures; *". . . be more humble then a blade of grass . . . more tolerant than a tree, Always give respect to others and expect none in return . . ."*(107) and *". . . I am the servant of the servant of the servant of the lotus feet of the master . . ."*(108) In the words of Kaliyaphani; *"Forgiveness then becomes effortless; "Forgive them Lord, they know not what they do." . . . that is not condescending but spoken from a platform of real knowledge."*(109)

"Forgiveness liberates the soul.
It removes fear.
That is why it is such a powerful weapon"(110)

STEP 8

RESOLVING

"Hatred does not cease by hatred, but only by love;
this is the eternal rule" (111)

One can see that while each of these steps represents a stage or aspect of personal development, the concepts are lightly touched upon and of course much abbreviated. Considered in more depth, they represent a single spirit that incorporates forgiving, resolving and healing, so that each is connected, united and working as one.

As we have observed this 'spirit', when living within us, frees us from the need to judge others. Forgiving becomes natural or more accurately totally irrelevant when there is nothing to forgive. While this understanding is elemental to all the major religions, Hinduism and its scion Buddhism, have perhaps best articulated it in their teachings through the ages. If we find and then live with balance and equilibrium, seeking resolution becomes as irrelevant as forgiveness, for neither will be really necessary. Kaliyaphani notes that the definition of resolution is to; *"release or bring back to the natural, relaxed state (and) is tied in with humility and peace."*

There is an obvious and inspiring example of these teachings living today, with an increasingly high international profile, while continuing the tradition of Gandhi and Mandela. As a committed Buddhist, the Burmese democracy leader Daw Aung San Suu Kyi gives us a practical focus in her life and utterances, forged in the constant brutality of politics. Consider, for example, what was said in November 2010, following Daw Suu Kyi's release from house arrest. She started the BBC interview by declaring that throughout her captivity, she had always felt free. By this she surely made clear her understanding that freedom is a state of mind and unrelated to any physical condition, while giving insight into the spirit of someone comfortable with 'humility and peace'. Of the military government she then went on; *"I am no danger to them, I mean them no harm"* and *"their right to justice is as strong as mine . . ."* In these words one could not wish for a clearer or more moving endorsement of the principles of non-violence, nor for that matter, a better example of a mature strategy towards achieving a resolution. What better definition of a statesman could we seek?

Later in the interview, Daw Suu Kyi tackled the notion of 'revolution' and its relationship to conflict resolution; *"A great change means a revolution"*. She defined revolution as simply *'radical change'*, thereby distancing herself from the necessity for violent change. The important point here and the key to achieving resolution, is the fearlessness that is implicit in this attitude. As she had said to Fergal Kean on her previous release from house arrest in 1995; *"Real freedom is freedom from fear"*. (112) Without this 'spirit', which is the confidence of inner not outer strength, resolution of any kind is much harder.

History has given us countless examples of violent revolution producing little more than the flip side of the same 'coin'. In each case, another form of oppressive regime replaced the former and little or no progress made towards conflict resolution or long-term peace. Consider the aftermath of the French, Russian or Chinese revolutions for clear evidence of this. With each, the violence after the upheaval equalled or actually exceeded anything before and if long-term peace was found, it was only following the eventual use of cooperative resolution methods. Violence, whether civil or military, is by definition, 'non-cooperative'. Proof of this can be found in the speeches of Lenin, who remonstrated; *"Only the dictatorship of the proletariat and the poor peasants is capable of smashing the resistance of the capitalists . . . Power to the Soviets - this is the only way to make further progress gradual, peaceful and smooth . . ."*(113) Falling over himself to sound the right note, Lenin did little more than fundamentally contradict himself, giving completely opposing notions. With the benefit of hindsight, we can see that Lenin was fired more by hate and revulsion than by the hope for anything *smooth* or *peaceful*.

Cooperation and resolution therefore must go hand in hand and this requires a maturity that strives to recognise some of the complex nuances of life. Without this willingness for understanding beyond the obvious, we are eternally condemned to primitive states of action and reaction. However humble the origins of our species, there is no reason to ignore the evolution that has occurred since, allowing us to reach new heights of cooperation and integration. These so-called 'primitive actions' are all too evident to the historian and modern observer alike. Peel away the thin layer of civil restraint and revealed beneath lies a terrifying range of extreme human behaviour. Unless we face up to these truths, we cannot set them aside and move beyond them. If, for example, we deny in our primitive makeup, the propensity to violent sexual domination, human sacrifice or even cannibalism, we will never be able to escape these tendencies within our societies.

Faced with the grim reality of some human behaviour and so many unresolved conflicts around the world, makes us aware of the urgent need to learn the skills to bring lasting harmony and peace, first within ourselves and then to others. We have seen that lasting resolution is impossible without forgiveness and yet crucial to any progress in human relations, is the need to remember. It is therefore important to make the distinction between forgiving and forgetting. To forgive is to move on towards understanding and cooperation, while to forget is to renounce all hope of progressing to a more enlightened future.

Much of the previous spirit relies on what has been called maturity but what exactly do we mean by this term? What are the qualities required to appreciate and act appropriately and without prejudice, bearing in mind the complexities of life? We have seen in Aung San Suu Kyi, an obvious balance and understanding. It is no doubt in part, the result of her worldliness and advanced education but to no less a degree, her inner faith and equilibrium. It could be argued that the search for truth via education is simply an attempt to return by the long route, to the truths inherent in simple faith and love. This notion is echoed in Kaliyaphani's bringing back to the *"natural, relaxed state"*. Jesus certainly felt the value of the simple, direct approach and found it in children; *"anyone who will not receive the kingdom of God like a little child will never enter it."*(114) This was undoubtedly a call to keep things modest and simple but not to advocate the cultivation of the juvenile or simplistic. We live in an age that appears to have taken Jesus' message too literally, so that we are surrounded by the cult of childhood and the general 'infantilisation' of much adult behaviour. This is a worrying development because we have lost sight of the importance of maturity. Evidence of this trend in society is evident in any action that forces individuals to submit to humiliating behaviour. Of course we speak here of consensual submitting, by those who consider it their obligation. There is plenty to be seen in the popular media, creating a culture of submission in the war of attrition against basic human dignity.(115)

When in 1922, Howard Carter finally discovered the tomb of Tutankhamen, he had hoped to learn something of the character of this three thousand year old boy king. In the end, he had to declare; *"The mystery of his life still eludes us, the shadows move but the dark is never quite dispersed."*(116) That Tutankhamen had come to the throne at nine, had proved to Carter his royal status, for by what other means could he have taken control of Egypt's empire? With documented evidence of powerful figures around the throne at the time, one can understand Carter's eagerness to know to what extent the boy had been in control of himself and his realm. For while maturity may come with age, there is no guarantee that it will and equally, children can show a maturity well beyond their age, to shame many an adult. We can only conjecture the level of Tutankhamen's maturity, from the time he ascended the throne to his death at around eighteen. Had he possessed it, we can imagine what this 'maturity' would have meant in practice. He would have observed and listened carefully to his advisors and then made up his own mind. He would have been prepared to reassess his opinion in the light of fresh evidence and alter course as required. He would have sought the skills to know when to hold fast and when to yield. Yes, these are skills that may require experience but they can also reflect just as much an attitude of mind. History gives us many an example of those with great experience who never gained such maturity. But while with Tutankhamen the mystery eludes us still, when we come in contact with it, it's not difficult to identify this maturity.

The risk is that in our eagerness to recapture the simplicity of childhood, we lose site of the nature of responsible, positive behaviour and the need for it in the world today. If the very word *responsibility* should suggest stuffy inhibition and make one want to reach for the bottle, then perhaps the point is made. Good judgement of circumstances and actions, without the need to judge individuals, therefore becomes an important attribute in resolving issues. It is an important and often difficult balancing trick. As the Koran states; *"Never let your enmity for anyone lead you into the sin of deviating from justice. Always be just: that is closest to being God-fearing."*(117) No wonder traditional religions, with their emphasis on accountability and sobriety often appear to be fighting a rear guard action. And perhaps it is no less surprising that many today are actively seeking these ancient disciplines in a backlash against a contemporary culture of indifference.

How might one recognise this maturity in others? Of course, there are many possible indicators but there is a simple test that proves the 'fitness' of an individual's spirit and that is an understanding of the importance of the spirit itself. If for example, we judge the validity of something purely on material appearance, perhaps the colour of skin, clothing or sexual orientation, then that spirit is not recognised. If we judge everything on its merits and true value, in other words the spirit behind the form, then problem resolution becomes much more effective.

Of course, not everything in life can be resolved. Part of the importance of modesty is recognising limitations. This essential attribute is key to a happy life and arguably a acknowledged definition of sanity. How much bloodshed could have been spared through history, had the world's leaders always appreciated their limitations both physical and spiritual. We are taught the virtue of fighting on; the sentiment of not 'quitting' but rarely the virtue of knowing when it is appropriate to yield. If we as individuals recognise and applaud the virtue of yielding when appropriate, we foster and encourage it in the wider world. By recognising our own limitations and being comfortable with them, we can be at peace with ourselves and those around us. But it is a balancing act and one that requires much application.

In the end resolution brings us back inevitably to the spirit of 'humility and peace'. This spirit prevails in both *rest* and *action* and makes sense once again of the notion of 'sportsmanship'. For in any endeavour we undertake, there need be no letup in effort or skill. But if everything is undertaken with humility and inner peace, then every act is an act of love. Playing with humility makes life a game of peace and winning irrelevant.

So lasting peace between people or nations requires the resolving of issues with a mature approach. If seeking resolution instead of conflict becomes the natural state, then peace evolves as a way of living. If conflicts are not resolved on an on-going basis, then violent solutions are sought. A suitable comparison might be the notion that '*A healthy body will eliminate constantly*', as considered in the Healing step. Without regular release of the 'toxins' of dispute, matters escalate into uncontrollable violence. Then the baser instincts of humanity are unleashed and the ensuing cost is immeasurable, as countless war survivors bear witness.

"If might is right, then love has no place in the world.
It may be so, it may be so.
But I don't have the strength to live in a world like that"(118)

STEP 9

LEADING

*"I suppose leadership at one time meant muscles;
but today it means getting along with people"*(119)

It is always possible and often easier to argue against an idea than make the effort to support and act upon it. After all, such adversarial skills are the basis of democracy and the living of advocates and 'agents'. In the same way, we can always choose to view life's glass as half empty. When half full it carries the same amount of water but forms the opposite approach and with wholly different consequences. In life, this is as much about exploring the problems which *"unite us, instead of belabouring those problems which divide us."*(120)

Viewing the glass as half full is an important concept in leadership. Where so much is subject to interpretation, single-minded pursuit of an idea is a necessary characteristic. This is because there is often an endless variety of directions to pursue, any one with its merits and pitfalls and each vulnerable to the sceptic's attack. It is so often stated by society's successful that their single greatest attribute was dogged perseverance in the face of failure and Richard Branson's *"you fail if you don't try . . ."* attitude is typical.(121) This outlook sees optimism and energy as absolutely key to leadership. Everyone who has witnessed a great stage performance at close quarters will recall the apparent concentrated effort committed. This is a notion implicit in the expression *"Success is ten percent inspiration and ninety percent perspiration."*(122) Add to this mix the discipline and dedication also required for success and one realises the exaggerated primacy given to the myth of inspiration alone.

To understand this better let us consider the so-called 'X Factor'. Any television program attempting to discover new 'stars' destined for fame and fortune, hits a major problem in the form of the dictates of market forces. This imperative would have us believe only the few are naturally gifted and therefore predestined for greatness. The truth is that with greater encouragement to sing, dance or excel in any other field, we are surrounded by those with extraordinary gifts and potential. But in our commercially driven society, 'products' must be marketed as unique or precious to command attention and the financial returns anticipated.

One could illustrate this 'X Factor' phenomenon another way. Diamonds are not rare. They are useful in industry but arguably of little more beauty than cut glass. Their preciousness and value is otherwise built on the notion of exclusivity and because there are so many of them under the ground, the idea of their rareness has had to be commercially manufactured. A single company has gone to enormous lengths to stockpile diamonds and create the artificial demand. Actually, the same practice is standard in most commercial endeavours, where the inevitable movement is towards monopolisation. It has been no less the case within the arts. In the 1960s the oeuvre of Rembrandt was reassessed and dramatically decreased, so that many works previously considered by the master were demoted to his followers.(123) This may have left many collections much the poorer but it has also increased the value of the remaining 'authenticated' stock.

The important point here is that it is a spirit that forges leaders not a commodity. This is a principle worth bearing in mind when seeking worthy leaders or for that matter, the capable leader within oneself. As an illustration of this, consider the constant dilemma of HR departments. There are usually many applicants for a position able to meet the broad requirements. What the interviewer must ascertain is the character of the applicant and their ability to adapt, integrate and survive. Put another way, it is sometimes said that one should *seek not the perfect partner but the perfect relationship*. In reality, it is the spirit that counts, not society's cultivated heroes. And the ability to excel in one field or another can be found within each one of us, regardless of any particular aptitude.

Capitalism, the guiding principle of our day, needs markets and the bigger and more reliable the better. These are markets built on need and by inference the need for something we cannot supply ourselves. We grow up with the notion that we must crave a precious commodity held for us by others. Such an attitude for example, discourages singing in favour of passive listening and by assumption, to those more gifted. The problem with this culture as we have already seen, is the increasing tendency to passivity, where we are all encouraged to become mere consumers. A gulf grows between we the 'enfeebled masses' and the supposed geniuses we worship. The resulting danger is that failing to understand our own worth, only fosters a gnawing and pernicious sense of frustration as we lose control of our destinies.

You could say that thus far this step has literally been about 'stepping up to the mark'. Doing this might well involve us in the management of a position of accepted authority. But it could as effectively revolve around unofficial instances with family or friends or as we have seen, simply a reflection of one's own attitude and outlook. As Mother Teresa put it; *"Do not wait for leaders; do it alone, person-to-person."*(124)

It is worth stressing that the *spirit* understood here, is closely related to the notion of *free will*. It is possible to argue that with the limitations of physical and mental competence, our free will is somewhat hypothetical and that we actually have very little capacity to change our own lives. One might observe a young, apparently fit beggar on the street and regret the impoverishment of the mind, rather than the purse, that keeps them sitting by the kerbside. But to deny in all humans, that part of us that is free to act independently and make decisions, is to condemn us to the slavery of circumstance. It also sets a dangerous precedent, where we are excused responsibility for our actions and any accountability for the cost. For, whatever creed we might choose to follow and however deprived our circumstances, we have to appreciate our own responsibilities and how they impact upon our communities and beyond. This spirit was memorably articulated in the poem by William Henley, quoted in the recent film about

Nelson Mandela; *"I thank whatever gods may be, for my unconquerable soul (for) I am the master of my fate, I am the captain of my soul."*(125) The abrogation of personal responsibility has of course an enormous impact on our communities, but society must equally ensure that responsibility means accountability. For a society without accountability is destined for anarchy.

It's too easy to see will or strength in terms of the domination of others but as we have seen, the use of the word spirit, suggests inner not outer strength. It is hard to know what it is about the air in South Africa but another great 20th century leader M Gandhi - who lived there for twenty years - put it succinctly; *"Strength does not come from physical capacity. It comes from an indomitable will."*(126) And this takes us back to the constant mantra of those who excel in their field; their belief in themselves and perhaps the optimism that kept them going through thick and thin to eventual triumph.

Unconquerable souls and *indomitable wills* does sound somewhat inflexible but in a true leader this is surely anything but the case. Yes, there will be a constant inner strength but there will also be awareness of the 'flux of life' that requires constant flexibility. The pull towards inflexibility in leaders is as strong as that drawing commerce towards monopoly. This fact makes flexibility combined with authority much harder than one might suppose. It is a challenge requiring constant vigilance and great effort. However, like everything else, with practice as well as the systems in place to promote it, flexibility can become a way of life for the mind and not just the body.

Flexibility in this sense is critical if we are to become aware of our own weaknesses and vulnerabilities and all the previous steps have helped us towards this goal. It is a poor leader that is not aware of themselves and those around them in this respect and able to adapt according to the changing world around them. So a good leader must be able to make space, for without it there can be no communication. They must also listen or they cannot learn, while at the same time avoiding being too easily swayed from the intended path. They must learn to heal for the sake of progress and have respect in order to build bridges towards resolution, cooperation and understanding.

This flexibility requires great concentration, without which we cannot judge situations to the best of our ability. Situations change and a good leader is able to change their judgement accordingly. But it is hard and most of us will naturally dodge the greater effort discernment requires and avoid that *"road less travelled."*(127) It requires admitting to mistakes and maintaining an element of vulnerability. The real flexibility comes from knowing when to stand firm and when to yield; when to show your strength and when your vulnerability. We know these characteristics when we hear them. The third president of the United States, Thomas Jefferson indicated his awareness of them in his inaugural address: *"I ask so much confidence only as may give firmness and effect to the legal administration of your affairs. I shall often go wrong through defect of judgment . . . I ask your indulgence of my own errors, which will never be intentional . . ."*(128)

This flexibility is entirely the result of inner strength. The vulnerability may feel like weakness but it is a fact of life that while we may not be aware of our own inner strength, it is always apparent to others. It is this inner force, this spirit that has the most profound effect on others. It is an extraordinary moment of maturity to realise that by simply altering one's own position, all around must change theirs too. It can be said therefore, that by taking control of oneself and thereby exuding inner strength, one changes everything. Through perhaps the smallest electromagnetic change in the brain, in the world beyond, nothing can remain the same.

If this notion appears something of a miracle, it is with good reason. For it works beyond the realm of vision and material perception and is very near to a definition of pure love. It is without fear, as a smile given to a complete stranger must not fear the consequences. It allows us to act and not react, to be a rock of strength against a turbulent sea. *"As we are liberated from our own fear, our presence automatically liberates others."*(129) Now as individuals with a strong spirit, we can each lead the way towards peace.

There is a somewhat sobering measure of the ultimate realisation of leadership skills and an indication of their power. Many of the greatest exponents of non-violence, far from dying in indifferent obscurity, have been the victims of violent assassination, so dangerous were their ideas to the dominating forces of the time.(130) And many with lower profiles have suffered greatly by having ruffled the feathers of the powerful. Leadership is about putting your head above the parapet, where it is exposed, being prepared to disagree with your friends and risk alienation or derision. But more than anything through leadership one demonstrates what one 'is' though inner strength, not by the power one 'has'. More than managers, leaders must demonstrate; *"Security, sense of identity and confidence based on faith in what one is, on one's need for relatedness, interest, love, solidarity with the world around us, instead on one's desire to have, to possess, to control the world, and thus become the slave of one's possessions."*(131)

> *"I have learned that a strong man has no need of power and a weak man is destroyed by it"*(132)

STEP 10

PEACE

"Peace starts with a smile"(133)

The previous step saw good leadership as a spirit of collaboration towards a single goal; a recognised aim considered important to all. Mother Teresa, again puts it unambiguously; *"If we have no peace, it is because we have forgotten that we belong to each other."* For her it was simple, it was the obligation of each of us to start the process that moves us always towards the spirit of peace and the state of peace, as they are fundamentally linked. *"Every time you smile at someone"* she wrote, *"it is an action of love, a gift to that person, a beautiful thing."*(134)

Much has been written about the new philosophy of cooperation and better integration. Out of the trauma of the twentieth century came the philosophy of *"Small is Beautiful."*(135) E F Schumacher saw a less competitive society, striving towards a sustainable existence as the only sane way forward. He famously wrote; *"Wisdom demands a new orientation of science and technology towards the organic, the gentle, the non-violent, the elegant and beautiful"*. More recently the likes of Fritjof Capra and Ken Wilber have attempted to outline a new understanding that sees all endeavours and disciples as united in a mutually dependent whole. Wilber encouraged movement towards a life of greater cooperation through; *"integral transformation practice"*;(136)　He believed not just in spiritual integration but what he called *Integral* politics, business, education and medicine. Cooperation would mean moving on from the post-modern *pluralistic relativism*, where we simply recognise our differences and remain separate, to one where we appreciate and enjoy our similarities and associations.

There is now undoubtedly a modern movement away from the hopelessness of post-modernism towards appreciating the connectivity of all life and the meaning that exists if we choose to recognise it. It deplores the dis-functioning that occurred at the point of the cold scalpel of 18th century reasoning (137) and continued unchecked into the modern age.　Instead, the world is understood with a fresh scientific language almost Biblical in its poetic vision.(138)

We have seen the importance of a positive attitude in guiding our actions and their effects, and certainly this cannot be exaggerated. Tolstoy spoke of the futility of military strategy in the real theatre of war when it was usually impossible to understand what was actually ensuing from minute to minute.(139) The success of Napoleon he argued was not so much down to marshal genius, as his ability to inspire the courage that was the real deciding factor in any conflict. Tolstoy believed that in riding 'heroically' on a white charger, Napoleon was able to tap into and augment the natural strength of purpose of the soldiers under his command. It is this strength of mind after all, that has allowed vastly outnumbered forces to win the famous victories that history likes to remember.

But this then begs the question, why are men so keen to kill each other and risk so much themselves? After all, the logic of war is hard to defend. Tolstoy himself wrote; *"In all history there is no war which was not hatched by the governments, the governments alone, independent of the interests of the people, to whom war is always pernicious even when successful."* What is it in man - and it would appear to be predominantly men - that leads them still to turn on each other in senseless violence? Scientists who preach the dominance of the selfish gene will stress that part of male aggression that leads him to dominate others and show his power; the only quality it is said, that impresses females.

Many Christians and Muslims have been taught that the *just war*(140) makes it imperative that they fight to protect a way of life and more importantly, the vulnerable in need of protection. However this conveniently disregards the reality that in Islam the *jihad* is the imperative to protect the faith with 'striving' and not necessarily war. The prominent 13th century Christian theologian Thomas Aquinas set the tone while seeking to clarify the earlier doctrine of St Augustine. Firstly, Aquinas stated that a war must be to *'right a wrong'*. Surely with greater understanding of other cultures and ways of life, we are nowadays less inclined to dictate rights and wrongs, besides which, when was there ever a war fought on clear moral grounds? He also believed a war must always be considered winnable, which again is hard to predict without the benefit of hindsight. He wrote that the suffering caused by waging a war, should be less than that from not waging it. In other words the war should be "efficient" in terms of human suffering.(141) But it is now clear to us that the effects of war are not only very hard to predict but open to much debate, as has happened right through history. The more we hear the justifications for war, the more they appear the primitive rantings of a bygone age.

But having admitted they exist, there is no logic to following our baser instincts, if we really believe in the advantages of civilisation and the rule of law. For war finds a resolution by total domination. As Tolstoy wrote; "*All violence consists in some people forcing others, under threat of suffering or death, to do what they do not want to do.*" War is undoubtedly a base instinct that destroys the soul, as he also put it; "*War is so unjust and ugly that all who wage it must try to stifle the voice of conscience within themselves.*" As for the 'just war', the world was told that the recent wars in Iraq and Afghanistan were justifiable against the tyranny of dictatorship and extremism. But in 2007, the primate of the Anglican Church, The Archbishop of Canterbury said, in his usual measured language; "*One of the aspects of traditional just war theory is that you need to know what would count as a good end and how you would know when you have that and what to do then (but) I don't think we had that in place sadly. I don't think we knew what we would do next or what would count as our ending. And that is the tragedy.*"(142) The Western coalition forces in Iraq apparently saw no need to keep account of civilian deaths. But it is believed that 66,000 may have died since the invasion began, more than half the total deaths from the conflict.(143) It would appear that the cost of protecting our own vulnerability must be the 'vulnerable' of others. So even the basic precepts of Aquinas have been breached with impunity. But we will return to the

'Holocaust argument' and saving the vulnerable, when discussing the notion of preventative peace.

Considering solely the economic cost of war, much of the astronomical present day national debt of Britain alone is the result of the 20th century's two world wars. As of November 2010, the figure is put at £4.8 trillion, amounting to roughly £77,000 for each man, woman and child in the country. It is estimated that if all the property in the country were sold, a trillion would still be owing.(144) It is also estimated that by February 2010 the US alone had spent around $704 billion on the Afghanistan and Iraq invasions. Meanwhile, by June of 2010 the Afghan War was being termed "America's Longest War", breaking the record of the infamous Vietnam War. In a BBC documentary of the same name made in 2011, an Afghan Mullah is heard to say; *"We don't want this government, we don't want the Americans, we don't want the British. Your men are here for killing Afghans; your tanks are for killing; your cannons are here for killing; your planes are for killing . . . (The people here) have been imprisoned, killed or fled. The Taliban will be here soon after you have left. They don't kill us. It is you who have brought the things for killing."*

If the environment concerns you more than economics, then we should consider just one related aspect of the global cost of wars. Through history, nations have caused systematic and catastrophic deforestation specifically when waging war. According to Luke Hughes, an expert on sustainable forest management, the Spanish Armada alone required 4,000 trees for each of its 125 ships, resulting in the loss of around half a million trees. Then you must add to that each ship's requirement for timber wharfs and the barrels of provisions for the estimated 30,000 troops. Twentieth century sensitivities made no impression; *"The First World War was particularly devastating to British woods: every ammunition box, railway sleeper, rifle butt, trench lining, carriage wheel, gun carriage and fence post was made from timber. Britain's forests, like those of France, were totally denuded . . . An even more calculated approach was taken after WWII, when the Americans deliberately culled the forests in their zone of occupied Germany with the specific purpose of reducing German industrial potential."*(145)   As we know too well, the world wars did not *"end all war"*(146) and the environmental carnage has persisted at an alarming rate. Hughes continues; *"In the Korean War in the 1950s, 80% of the country's forests were clear-felled within 3 years, mostly for fuel and, since food was so short, clearance for agricultural land. In Vietnam, 44% of the forest was defoliated by bombs, bulldozers or Agent Orange."*

The true cost of war goes well beyond the environment, finance or the body count of combatants. It is impossible to realistically quantify the cost but then history has seldom bothered its attempt. How can we measure the trauma of war on civilians and soldiers alike; the long term psychological damage on whole communities; the economic cost; the environmental cost; the cost in lives lost since conflicts? UNISEF has kept a record of child deaths since the Vietnam War. In one village alone 300 children have lost their life and many more maimed or blinded just by landmines,(147) called by UNICEF; *"the most toxic pollution known to man."*(148) Finally, it was a huge disappointment to Churchill to realise the unexpected long-term cost of the Second World War. *"An Iron Curtain"*(149) split the nations of the world into two competing, distrusting and aggressive halves and set us on a course towards the risk of total annihilation.

No, war represents the complete breakdown of civilisation. Throughout history, it has been romanticised to encourage unsuspecting youths to venture their lives, until the truth dawns that they have been hoodwinked; "the *deception which is being practiced on them.*"(150) The hell of war then becomes apparent, innocence is shattered and lives destroyed by the experience; "*What branches grow out of this stony rubbish?*"(151) It represents the total breakdown of order because it wipes out the very things it sets out to protect; security, trust and culture. It leaves behind only anger and suffering; the seeds for subsequent conflict and so it goes on; a never-ending cycle of senseless stupidity. The soldier and poet Siegfried Sassoon became all too aware of the realities of the 1st World War. He wrote; "*. . . I have seen and endured the sufferings of the troops, and I can no longer be a party to prolong those sufferings for ends, which I believe to be evil and unjust. I am not protesting against the conduct of the war, but against the political errors and insincerities for which the fighting men are being sacrificed. Also I believe that I may help to destroy the callous complacence with which the majority of those at home regard the continuance of agonies which they do not share, and which they have not sufficient imagination to realise.*" A paratrooper who described the Second World War simply as 'hell' also remembered; "*When you're young, it sounds exciting, war; shooting people. It's not exciting at all, it's a dirty business.*"(152)

"*War is like a fire in the human community, one whose fuel is living beings*" states the Dalai Lama; "*Since armies are legal, we feel that war is acceptable; in general, nobody feels that war is criminal or that accepting it is a criminal attitude. In fact, we have been brainwashed. War is neither glamorous nor attractive. It is monstrous. Its very nature is one of tragedy and suffering.*"

But then he continues; "*After the officer in charge have given beautiful explanations about the importance of the army, its discipline and the need to conquer the enemy, the rights of the great mass of soldiers are most entirely taken away. They are then compelled to forfeit their individual will, and, in the end, to sacrifice their lives. Moreover, once an army has become a powerful force, there is every risk that it will destroy the happiness of its own country.*" (153)

Mohandas Gandhi wrote; "*Violent means will give violent freedom. That would be a menace to the world and to India herself*" and he would know. By living the pure Christian doctrine of non-violence, that diminutive figure was able to bring to its knees the awesome power of a great empire. Violence begets violence, knows only violence and thrives on violence. Empires survive by conflicts and without it they are rendered powerless. Gandhi proved this conclusively in India but history presents another clear example in the demise of the Roman Empire. Anyone who calls them self a follower of Christ, must understand the true nature of his ministry and his profoundly non-violent doctrine. Jesus declared; "*Do not resist an evil person*" but "*turn the other cheek.*" Not much to debate there, nor is there in any of his teachings for that matter. He taught that we should love our enemies, forgive those that sin against us, that the peacemakers were blessed and those that live by the sword, by the sword would die.(154)

While it is sometimes argued that St Paul the Evangelist changed the direction of Christianity after the death of Christ, the spirit of non-violence remained in his teaching. Perhaps Jesus did not rise from the dead but it is still an undeniable fact that he was not prepared to take up arms against the Romans and in his death, set a powerful precedent of non-violent action. History proves to us that the early Christians were pacifists and so represented a dangerous challenge to Roman society, built as it was on martial, stoic principles. It is hardly surprising then that pagan Rome so persecuted the early Christians, seeing them as a revolution against the patriarchal, macho beliefs that kept the Roman imperial machine in control. After all, it was no mean feat keeping that enormous, disparate empire from crumbling apart. And it is sometimes argued that it was the very adoption of Christianity by Emperor Constantine in 312 AD that started the process towards its eventual collapse in 410 AD. Perhaps the great irony here is that the last laugh was Rome's, in drawing Christianity into its lethal embrace, absorbing the 'punch' of the faithful and weakening Christian resolve in the process.(155)

If Christianity did break the Roman Empire, the execution of Jesus really was *"the greatest mistake ever made by Rome."*(156) It would also make this revelation the clearest endorsement of the teachings of Mohandas Gandhi. Gandhi wrote; *"Non-violence is the greatest force at the disposal of mankind. It is mightier than the mightiest weapon of destruction devised by the ingenuity of man."*(157) As previously mentioned, we have to see Gandhi as the shining light in the twentieth century, of early Christian teaching. One can't help wondering if there might be some truth in the assertion that Christ travelled East during his unrecorded years and came under oriental spiritual influence. The words of Gandhi could have equally come out of the mouth of Jesus; *"I am prepared to die, but there is no cause for which I am prepared to kill."*

There is perhaps one distinction we should make here and that is between military *aggression* and military *policing*. The Romans did not consider their presence in Palestine as that of an occupying force but simply in a *peacekeeping*, 'policing' capacity. Although to the Zealots fighting for freedom, the distinction would have seemed somewhat academic, it is a real one all the same. Whatever you choose to call your soldiers, it is within the spirit of intent that any justification can be made. It is generally the intention in 'policing' to keep the peace by non-aggressive means, while an army is used to impose national will by force. Of course there are times when police forces cross that line themselves. Yet, armies in peacekeeping roles would have been understood by Jesus as the comparatively benign Roman force with which he was familiar. This is of course in stark contrast to those times when Rome decided to unleash its full military force, such as against Palestine in 69AD.

So for the sake of argument we are back to that 'spirit', a spirit defined by intent. Even if that intent is considered a 'necessary evil' to provide security and peace, only the most wantonly naïve would deny what really ensues when war breaks out and the norms of human restraint are removed. Despite the glorification of war in our culture, history shows us that when governments decide on mobilisation, it invariably involves rape, torture, genocide and mass cultural destruction.(158) Some armies are trained in the art of restraint in the heat of conflict but any soldier will admit that this can be a very difficult discipline. Even the most highly trained army is unable to escape the shame of humanitarian lapses.

There is a famous adage, *"if you want peace, prepare for war"*(159) and is the regularly used argument in support of a very lucrative armaments industry.(160) The reality is that countries that build armies tend to use them, if only in an attempt to justify the cost. The United States now spends more on armament than the next eight of the world's great military powers. Far from preventing conflict, the US has bombed twenty-two countries since the end of the Second World War. In the Vietnam War alone, the US dropped more tonnage of bombs than all the countries involved in the Second World War combined. The argument for the 'just war' - the war to preserve freedom or for self-defence - would carry more weight if there wasn't always so obviously a motivation of national self interest. These interests range from the grabbing of land and resources to simply the fear of other countries and separate cultures. As Aung San Suu Kyi puts it; *"The gun is always there for use . . . we are convinced that the non-violent approach is best."*(161)

The so-called *War on Terror* and the invasions that followed is a perfect example of where the *intent* has lost credibility in the West. As a result, those involved in armed struggle against the West, attack civilians because they consider them responsible as voters in democracies that supported their governments in invading. If we live in a culture that accepts violent means as appropriate to solve international issues, then perhaps they have a point. Of course in turn, the terrorists forfeit all credibility by choosing violence themselves. When the World Trade Centre was attacked in 2001, the US won enormous sympathy and *"a moral victory before the world."*(162) But that valuable currency of goodwill was squandered by the decision to lash out in the Middle East, with dubious motives and little obvious forethought. The real tragedy is that the 'ghosts' of so many wars, often believing or hoping they were fighting a *war to end all wars*, appear to have had so little power to influence our attitudes to violence today. Besides which, we have to consider whether armed conflict serves our interests in any way. Using armies aggressively creates long lasting hatred, as we awaken to the myth that is the 'surgical strike'. But particularly since 9/11, it would appear that, as expressed by Fredrrik Heffermehl for the International Peace Bureau in Geneva, *"The military can no longer deliver the product we pay them for - security"*.

We have admitted the obvious; that it is impossible to measure the true cost of war. How for example, could we measure the financial cost alone of the Second World War, when it is hard enough to measure how many simply died? If a rough estimate can be made of say the cultural loss, it is impossible to gage the psychological cost. We are aware that war creates huge and long lasting trauma but what of the effect of the culture of violence on our attitudes and the psyche of our descendants? It is a clear example of society's schizoid thinking, where we tell our children to be gentle and loving to others, while engaging in remorseless aggression on those with whom we disagree. In war's defence, we are always told to measure the cost of the Second World War against the loss of life in the Holocaust and the loss of freedom as a result of defeat. We hear phrases such as a *'necessary evil'* or *'you have to be cruel to be kind'* but the simple truth is that two wrongs never make a right and that should be the guiding principle that makes peace the gold standard. The Second World War for all its costs - estimated to be around sixty million in lives alone (163) - did nothing to stop an estimated eleven million dying in the Nazi and other death camps, as part of the estimated forty million total civilian deaths. So the case for having gone to war to protect the vulnerable was apparently a very weak one. Yes, war brought parties to the negotiating table, but why not go there before the start?

A much more appropriate adage should be; *"Si vis pacem para pacem"; if you want peace, prepare for peace.*(164) Preparing for peace in wartime is obviously too late, it must be done constantly, as a way of life. That is to say, there are many other factors that placed the Jews in jeopardy during that war, including historic anti-Semitism and our reluctance to challenge it, as well as arguably some culpability on the part of Jews themselves. As for 'freedom', if you use the same methods as your enemy, you will be seen as no better than them. The freedom you preserve will be built on repression. It is also possible to argue that, if a nation is solid in its belief system, then it is impervious to subjugation following an invasion. We're talking here of course of the potential for passive resistance, where India under the guidance of Gandhi is the perfect proof of this phenomenon. The argument goes; if we value our culture and principles, why should we fear the rhetoric of a Hitler? Democracies today believe that such evil principles need not be unduly censored, so they may be tested in the fires of reason, found wanting and be appropriately laughed out. You fight what you fear and there is surely hope when a President of the United States can say; *"we proved once more that the true strength of our nation comes not from the might of our arms or the scale of our wealth, but from the enduring power of our ideas; democracy, liberty, opportunity, and unyielding hope."*(165)

Many who agree with this sentiment, will at the same time, have no problem wearing their poppy and remembering the immense bravery and commitment of soldiers in the past or current serving personnel. Belief in peace is not an insult to their memory or professionalism, although it is often suggested as such by those trying to galvanise support for a war. It is not unpatriotic to follow the teachings of Christ and as we have seen, the core doctrine of all the major religions. While admittedly individual combatants do have some responsibility for their part in wars, in reality the decisions made are usually much more corporate and in democracies, of course, involve a whole nation. Besides which, we should not automatically assume anyone carrying a gun is not themselves vulnerable. History's high percentage of child soldiers aside, soldiers can also be as naive and deprived as the rest of us.

Preparing for peace, means putting peace at the centre of our cultural belief system. The steps we have taken so far have prepared us mentally for an attitude of reason and balanced harmony. It is also necessary to then build a society that is adverse to violence and aggression. This is not to stifle competition and physicality in our children but to rediscover the significance of 'sportsmanship'. That is the spirit that enjoys the competing but is not desperate to win and doesn't have to defeat. Many will know the characteristic in exponents of the martial arts, that allows them - with the aid of Buddhist meditation - to release great energy, without any aggression. It is a novel concept in the West, where aggression works hand in hand with the emotional need to win and thereby triumph over others.

If we have within us inner strength of character, we will not need to win and will enjoy a confidence in ourselves that allows our barriers to fall. A sense of security and trust given off by us is bound to inspire the same qualities in others. Mikhail Gorbachev's open-handed approach to the West was the overriding factor that allowed the great rapprochement and ultimately the end of the

Cold War.(166) That the USSR was suffering economic hardship at the time is true but it doesn't change the basic principle that a non-aggressive approach to others aids a non-aggressive response. It is a law of nature, seen constantly in animal behaviour and in humans was expressed in its purest form by the spirit of Gandhi; *"For peace has its victories more glorious than those of war. The non-violent method would have meant no abject surrender. It would have confounded all modern tactics of war, indeed rendered them of no use."*(167)

In this respect, we also behave within nature's laws. Anyone who has spent time working with those inclined to violence, will know that if the individual is approached with a body language of openness, then they are far less likely to act aggressively in response. Of course, following this doctrine is not to exclude the use of defence, for there are times when it is simple expedience to offer some kind of resistance, to avoid harm. But there is a line that could be crossed, that turns defence into offence and where then 'offence' is taken. So by remaining open with those around us, we show our defencelessness and by our trust, we also show our strength.

Putting peace at the centre of our cultural belief system means both having the right spirit individually but also underpinning it with national laws. Some cultures are very quick to condemn what is considered excessive sexual license in the media, yet quite indifferent to the many kinds of violence represented. If we condemn racism and all forms of prejudice, why do we not put some limits on violence itself? As an example of this, a father in Pakistan recently complained about the video games played by his Muslim son. Because these games were made in the West, they continually represented Muslims as the enemy. His son spent his evening playing games with names such as; "Muslim Massacre". What can be the effect of this indoctrination on a child and what does it say to the Muslim world about understanding and tolerance?(168)

We need a society that insists on peaceful practice at all times. This needs to include violent demonstrations in our own lands as well as our disputes with other countries; *"If you want to make peace with your enemy, you have to work with your enemy. Then he becomes your partner."*(169) We need to recognise and uphold international laws and conventions as sacrosanct. In the same way that police are given respect in individual countries for providing security and enforcing order, the United Nations peacekeeping forces need the same respect. The blue helmets should carry the authority of a global wide consensus and with it, be without reproach as the guardians of global peace. It is a question of holding fast to the lessons of the twentieth century and remembering the conciliatory words of President Sadat; *". . . no one can build his happiness at the expense of the misery of others . . . the call for permanent and just peace, based on respect for the UN resolutions, has now become the call of the whole world."*(170) In the spirit of this approach, there must be obvious accountability, so that violence is dealt with, whether from violent civil unrest or the vigilante opportunism of the perpetrators of illegal wars. Governments must know that the unilateral invasion of another country is the simple definition of an illegal war, with consequences sufficient to be a deterrent. The words of Gandhi come to mind; *"Liberty and democracy become unholy when their hands are dyed red with innocent blood."*(171)

Governments as well as individuals need integrity. Centuries of a commerce driven culture has resulted in an unhealthy reliance on 'agents' to undertake on our behalf everything we think we can't or won't. These agencies are without full discernment because they tend to operate within narrow directives, for example, a government on behalf if it's electorate or even a barrister as counsel. Without integrity - if you like, the simple willingness to disagree with your friends when appropriate - we are ruled and controlled by small-minded 'pressure-groups'. When Iraq attached Iran in 1980, it was in direct breach of UN Security Council resolution 479 but the international community initially did nothing. The simple reason for this was explained by the US Secretary of State Madeleine Albright; *"The thing that is so cynical about this, is that there was a certain point when all five permanent members of the security council were providing arms to both sides of the war"*.

However, one cannot stress enough the importance of that right spirit within each individual. Without it, no amount of national laws or international resolutions will make the blindest bit of difference, for we are ingenious at finding ways to break rules and flaunt the spirit if not the letter of the law. In her famous 'Freedom from Fear' speech,(172) Aung San Suu Kyi spoke of the need for a *'revolution of the spirit'*, without which *"the forces which produced the iniquities of the old order would continue to be operative, posing a constant threat to the process of reform and regeneration."* The right spirit has to be courageous both in thought and in the face of possible oppressive regimes. *"It is not power that corrupts but fear. Fear of losing power corrupts those who wield it and fear of the scourge of power corrupts those who are subject to it."*

Many of us have never been in a situation that requires such courage but are grateful for the example of those who have inspired us. Gandhi would have agreed that non-violence can hurt, can require enormous effort, pain and endurance and it is anything but a soft option. As we saw in Step 1, there are times when the best option is to do nothing but non-violence does not necessarily require inaction.(173) Daw Suu Kyi, is stirred by Gandhi's example when she says; *"It is not enough merely to call for freedom, democracy and human rights. There has to be a united determination to persevere in the struggle, to make sacrifices in the name of enduring truths, to resist the corrupting influences of desire, ill will, ignorance and fear."*(174)

Daw Suu Kyi's *"revolution of the spirit"* could equally be described as an evolution of the mind; a moving on to more advanced thinking and what Ken Wilber called *"An integral vision."*(175) This spirit has to be informed, flexible and courageous to make bold and honest judgments and not be confined by prejudice and selfishness. As we have seen, violent political revolutions usually flip to produce the dark side of the same 'coin'. This was the experience of France in the eighteenth century and Russia and China in the twentieth. Education and a loving culture are the vital ingredients to take that spirit forward. But no amount of education can compensate for a culture that is not built on love and understanding. As one might expect, nations don't live in love and understanding with each other and then simply flip in times of war. War is ignorance and hate by other means. 'Cold wars' are fought all the time between governments in so called 'peacetime' and playground alliances seem to require secrets and constant jostling for shifting friendships. In this immature environment (of what Aldous Huxley called 'boy-gangsters'), war is simply the continuance of the wrong *spirit*, with even less constraint and as we have seen, invariably none at all.

Many argue that there is a natural progression in the development of humans away from the egotism of childhood towards the *universal care* that embraces *humanity as a whole.* The psychologist Howard Gardner stated; *"the whole course of human development can be viewed as a continuing decline in egocentrism."* This maturity allows us to embrace the world and care for it, rather than feel a victim of it. Or in the words of Ken Wilber, to; *"move from ethnocentric to world-centric, from dominator social hierarchies towards meritocracies, from duty to dignity."*(176) Religions will not satisfy the needs of mature humans if they are not able to embrace the whole world with their love but simply remain ethnocentric. Fortunately, this is a growing understanding, championed by the likes of the Dalai Lama in an attempt to promote stronger notions of universal compassion and responsibility and the realisation of our interdependency.(177)

When Charles Darwin prepared to declare to the world that species are not immutable and published 'The Origin of Species', he said it was like *"confessing a murder"*. In some respect, declaring oneself committed to non-violence, feels much the same. Even today, it is considered a threat to the same Romano-martial and macho culture that is still tribal in its attitudes and naturally hostile to anything 'foreign'. One thinks of the utterances of George Patten during the Second World War; *". . . a real man will never let his fear of death overpower his honor, his sense of duty to his country and his innate manhood. Battle is the most magnificent competition in which a human being can indulge."*(178) The Philosopher Bertrand Russell summed up the hypocrisy in the statement; *"Patriots always talk of dying for their country but never of killing for their country."* In total contrast, there are the moving words of Martin Luther King from perhaps the best-remembered speech of the last century; *"In the process of gaining our rightful place we must not be guilty of wrongful deeds. Let us not seek to satisfy our thirst for freedom by drinking from the cup of bitterness and hatred. We must ever conduct our struggle on the high plane of dignity and discipline. We must not allow our creative protest to degenerate into physical violence. Again and again we must rise to the majestic heights of meeting physical force with soul force."*(179) A notion of mature *dignity* is developing here, where dignity and integrity aspire to a higher spiritual realm.

Until, as collective human beings, we are able to break free of these baser constraints, we will never be able to live in peace. There is no reason why if nations can keep a semblance of order within their borders, international law cannot achieve the same. We have seen that the path of non-violence is not an indication of weakness but of prevailing strength, requiring faith, understanding and conviction. We need to be constantly vigilant to ensure violence and prejudice are always brought to book, whether rioting students or the perpetrators of illegal wars. We must fight the political incentive to always agree with our friends. These are the qualities that provide the best defence for a worthwhile society against attack, not the violence of counter-attack or even the so-called 'pre-emptive strike', amounting to little more than unprovoked aggression. *"Thus to provide the people with the protective coolness of peace and security, rulers must observe the teachings of the Buddha. Central to these teachings are the concepts of truth, righteousness and loving kindness. It is government based on these very qualities that the people of Burma are seeking."*(180)

In the words of another Nobel Peace Prize winner; *"What will the legacy of this vanishing century be? . . . Surely it will be judged, and judged severely in both moral and metaphysical terms . . . So much violence, so much indifference."*(181) What is required here is not a vain hope of a vague path towards some future utopia. There is a chronically overdue imperative to act now, for the immediate signs are not looking good. Nature threatens to provide catastrophic tests of man's ability to work together in adversity, extremist forces - both democratically elected and not - threaten to unleash forces with the potential to wipe humanity off the face of the globe. The while, commercial, spiritual and political uncertainties, risk erupting into widespread civil unrest. Never has there been a greater need for the strength of the proactive, non-violent leader, to stand up and be counted. As a scientist confronted by the realities of the modern age, Oppenheimer put it in stark terms but understood the required spirit; *". . . I think it is true to say that atomic weapons are a peril, which affect everyone in the world, and in that sense a completely common problem . . . I think that in order to handle this common problem there must be a complete sense of community responsibility . . . the point I want to make, the one point I want to hammer home, is what an enormous change of spirit is involved . . . We cannot forget our dependence on our fellow men."*(182)

Loving kindness or *"Soul Force"*, call it what you will and arrived at it by whatever discipline your culture dictates, is clearly the greatest ingredient to lasting peace in the world, for individuals and nations alike. Each of us needs to admit our powerlessness in the face of truth; feel the '*gap*' in which that truth resides; order our lives so that peace and harmony are present when we are active as well as relaxed and seek to love our fellow human beings, constantly and with all our hearts.

This can only happen - as recognised by the wise throughout history - when we free ourselves from the slavery of craving to own and dominate. Whether as individuals or as humanity, our only hope for survival on this planet, is to constantly practice the loving mode of being and to inspire a new age of cohesion, cooperation and integration between us all.

"A small body of determined spirits fired by
an unquenchable faith in their mission
can alter the course of history"(183)

CONCLUSION

THE SIMPLE TRUTH

". . . So non-violence to her is about love"(184)

The more we say the less is said and I have promised a simple, clear read, so it is time to sum up all that has been considered and reach our conclusion.

Through the testaments of the great philosophies and religions of the world, we have seen that in essence they all share the same principles. They may become compromised by greed and ignorance in time's political cauldron but strip away the layers of fat and they throb with a single energy. It is surely an enormous relief to discover that a competing 'marketplace' of conflicting ideologies does not divide humanity. For all agree that the material world drags us down, that hate should give way to love, fear to faith and conflict to forgiveness and peace. We can choose to fear and hate what we do not understand or alternatively feel the joy in knowing that goodness is universally accepted and has been a gold standard throughout history.

Again, with negligible distinctions - usually adding richness in diversity - we can see the methods for finding 'joy' as also universally accepted. No culture will deny the importance of breathing, listening or good health, nor the fundamental attributes of a true leader. We can take just as much comfort through knowing that by the application of a disciplined life following simple steps, we can effect a complete change in ourselves. But just as importantly, we can see that when we ourselves change and find that inner peace, even in the tumult of our lives, then all around us must also change. This too is a supremely exciting revelation because it informs us that we really are the masters of our own lives and crucially important to the world around us. Even when it feels most like it, we are never islands of isolation, unable to affect an impact on our surroundings. On the contrary, we are part of a rich tapestry, where all the elements are interwoven and interrelated. Tug on one thread and you will affect all the others around. This is true not only for humans but also of course in the way we relate to the natural world; we are not on top of it, nor for that matter oppressed by it but truly 'in it' and part of it.

This is important because hours spent on the metaphorical meditation mat will bring us no closer to inner peace, unless we are at peace with the world of which we are an *integral* part. So our peace must be a constant thread even when we are at our busiest; finding peace within our family, our community and beyond, that incorporates all people and all things. For it will be the proof of our love and understanding, our tolerance and our knowing that we are without enemies and are at peace with the universe.

However, I hear you say; that's all very well but humans are eternally politic and we live in a world of conflict and confusion. How is one individual to change a world so apparently - and now scientifically proven to be - set on a hopeless course of self-destruction? Be realistic I hear you cry! But let us not forget that deep well of wisdom from which this book draws its countless quotes; wisdom across cultures and throughout the ages. All point to the primacy and naturalness of the state of peace and the importance of non-violence in the resolution of conflict. They speak as one, of the need for love and the necessity of forgiveness as the requisite for a healthy and sustainable life.

So we must ask ourselves, why is civilization no longer civil? Have we lost the ability to see our own culture of violence and how it has shaped us and our surroundings? Are we perhaps part of the problem and can now imagine nothing else? If, as we have seen, we can transform our spirit for the better and change the world around us, could we not as easily have adopted an aggressive and dominating spirit, to which we are now enslaved both physically and psychologically? Let us consider the world in which we live. Our modern industrial culture saw its inspiration in the martial brutality of the Roman Empire. While Rome looked to Greece for its inspiration, it knew itself to be an inferior culture in all but its ability to dominate others. Homophobia for example, was always an indicator of the brutalising of male role models. It was endemic in Roman society but of little concern to ancient Greece. Only an insecure, emotionally subjugated male, fears the capacity to love another man. And that distorted perspective has survived, even flourished under misguided Christian and other dogmas and lives today, two thousand years later, alongside the same imperialist, dominating violence that has been our inheritance. For further proof, consider the facts of sexual violence today as another indicator of the same underlying social aggression.(185) Our culture functions with apparently bafflingly high levels of sexual abuse. It thrives within the family against the very children parents are meant to love so much, in communities, in prisons, the army and now almost everywhere as systematic torture and ethnic repression. There is an assumption that these acts are driven by lust or sexual attraction, but experience tells us that they are more about violence, anger and the need to dominate others, whether male or female; it makes little difference.

Western society looked back to Rome for a sense of justice and a sophisticated system of checks and balances but the best intentions are always open to abuse and dissipation. Rome, perhaps the victim of its own success, became as much about conquest and suppression. We have seen how by taking on the mantle of Christianity, Rome both removed the threat from the non-violent movement and compromised that movement's very own spirit. We have seen a 'Roman' Christian church develop over the centuries, that some see as having fitted in well with the pagan spirit of the age but with an unclear relationship with the core values of Jesus Christ. For two thousand years a careful path has been sort through any remaining spark of truth to reinforce the dominance of nation states and their dogmatic ideologies. Each generation has tortured and burned any who did not tow the 'orthodox' line. A loving, peaceful spirit and in particular, the appreciation of the non-material, have suffered in the wake of repression and intolerance.

On these 'pagan' foundations grew an industrial age with an imperative and ability to own, develop, dominate and control on a new and unimagined scale. It fostered *The Great Promise* of unlimited material growth and freedom and it resulted in an explosion of imperial and commercial fervour. This has shaped who we are and how we act as never before. In the words of Erich Fromm, the *"assumption was, that what was good for the "system", for big corporations, was good for man, as man was innately egotistic, selfish & greedy, therefore man was being 'natural'."* (186) In one sense, we have all become kings and therefore vulnerable to the corrupting influence of power and material wealth. When accepting his 1952 Nobel Price for Peace, Albert Schweitzer declared; *". . . it must shake up our conscience that we become all the more inhuman the more we grow into supermen."* Grabbing, reaching, dominating everything around, we have been insensitive to the suffering around us, allowing us to justify incredible brutality, often in the very name of peace. Fromm saw the consequence of this 'scorched earth' existence; *"We hesitate not at all at leaving our own descendants this plundered earth as their heritage."* (187)

Undeniably, the capacity of our species for aggression is as old as that of any other related species. But while once is was an existential part of living in harmony with nature, it has now become a constant attitude of mind where nature's only parallel is that associated with the desperation of caged animals. A simple, natural life, as the study of 'primitive' cultures has shown, produces a gentle spirit. Such tribes can still be found in the wildest jungles of the globe and their softly spoken gentleness is extraordinary to behold. (188) Today, it is the modern mind that is itself in constant war with itself and others, so that despite the absence of any actual cause to fight, it can see nothing but conflict and in that spirit, cannot help but perpetuate it. *"It is ironic"* declares the Dalai Lama *"that the more serious problems emanate from the more industrially advanced societies. Science and technology have worked wonders in many fields, but the basic human problems remain. There is unprecedented literacy, yet this universal education does not seem to have fostered goodness, but only mental restlessness and discontent instead."* (189)

We must be in no doubt about what we mean by modern society. It harbours the disease of affluence, where excessive desire blinds us into ignorance and an illogical aggression. As a disease it respects no classes, borders or timescale. It grew out of all proportion with the explosion of capacity and competition generated by the industrial revolution that followed the ascendancy of Europe. But it has spread far and wide and now possesses many a culture once devoted to spiritual or 'social-ist' principles. It infects the mind and debilitates the spirit of all but the strongest and it fights with many a powerful weapon. If we have known little better, we cannot see the malaise that grips our very beings or fully appreciate the anger and frustration in our own homes, on our streets and roads and every forum of self-expression. A vast industry perpetuates myths to deliberately confuse our thinking, through the sophisticated propaganda of advertising and the mass media. In stark terms, Tavener *sees us in; "the grips of a global catastrophe, a global nightmare . . The ordinary people out there - there is something missing in their lives, they can't articulate exactly what it is, but they are searching."* He perceives us as having forgotten our noble 'divine' origins; *"Having in our minds desanctified ourselves, we have also desanctified the natural world in our minds. This self-image and world view have their origin in our loss of memory, in our forgetfulness of who we are, and in our fall to a level of ignorance and stupidity that threatens the survival of our race."* (190)

We have come to see our brand of violence as right and our 'enemies' as evil. We have declared war on terror and ignored our own 'axis of ignorance'. Much of the terror that occupies the modern mind was forged in the many apocalyptic wars of the twentieth century. During the Second World War Adolf Hitler was perceived as the evil enemy and Winston Churchill the brave defender of freedom. But Gandhi noted; *"It is very difficult to judge when both sides are employed in violence which side deserved to succeed."* For though he respected the democratic principles that had given him education and opportunities, he also believed; *"The clean end of imperialism is likely to be the end of Fascism and Nazism. This can only be done if and when Britain sheds the gains of perhaps the most organized and successful violence the world has ever known."* But here's the rub, in 1942 Gandhi went on to declare; *"(Britain) will not be able to retrace her steps after out-Hitlering Hitler in war. The last war is a resounding lesson. Her victory, if attained, will be a snare and a delusion. I know mine is a voice in the wilderness. But it will some day ring true."*

That chilling prophecy has come home to haunt us. We now cannot see the truth, even when it stares us in the face. *"War on Terror"* - we know the phrase is laughable but we appear powerless to contradict it personally or through our institutions. Even the former Director General of MI5, Baroness Manningham-Buller conceded she; *"didn't believe the so-called 'War on Terror' was winnable in a military sense."* (191) We talk of *"Weapons of Mass Destruction"* wielded by the so called *'axes of evil'*, while forgetting that it was democracies that actually used the WMDs of the A bomb, Zyklon B and Agent Orange. Democracies supported the Taliban against the Russian invasion of Afghanistan and then Saddam Hussein against the perceived threat of the Ayatollahs in Iran. In fact democracies have been more than happy to maintain cordial relations with most of the extremist dictatorships of the world, supporting their regimes and supplying them with arms. When the Middle East blew up into civil unrest in early 2011 and the British Prime Minister David Cameron went out there on a diplomatic mission, he was accompanied by what the British Media described as *"a caravan of British arms dealers."* Whatever the crisis, it would appear it is always business as usual and the business is good. The British defence industry is currently worth around £35 billion and employs 300,000.(192)

The truth is, however much we demonise the likes of Hitler and Gaddafi, we have to recognise the violence within ourselves. Winston Churchill, for all his brilliance and charisma, was by no means a lover of peace. How could he be when born at Blenheim Palace, a stupendous - and dangerously beautiful - monument to national military 'glory'.(193) Gandhi may not have mentioned Churchill's name in saying; *"A warrior lives on his wars whether offensive or defensive. He suffers a collapse if he finds that his warring capacity is unwanted."* But it is no coincidence that in 1945 Churchill admitted; *"I feel so lonely without a war."*(194)

Churchill personified the British 19th Century aspiration to world dominance, through power and military glory. But he was also a champion of freedom of speech and understood well the great limitations of democracy. If Britain today really does consider him the greatest of their kind, then they must surely to some extent, endorse his principles and methods. With a society reared on this heady cocktail of empire and the domination of lesser mortals, is it really surprising he is hero-worshiped and we easily forget his violent temper, prejudices and tendencies towards rash and sometimes disastrous military decisions? Churchill's reputation rests on his dogged defence of the principle of democracy, apparently at any cost. But should we view democracy as the ultimate panacea? Should we protect it at any cost, especially if that cost is countless innocent lives, the breaking of spirits and wholesale destruction of cultures? If we value in democracy its free speech, peaceful dialogue and civility, do we not lose all we treasure most when we fight with total abandon in our attempt to preserve them?

Many a 'small voice' has spoken of another way; the way of non-violence and this is not the wishful thinking of naive idealists. One might view Gandhi as an isolated maverick but one of his great inspirations was the mighty Emperor Ashoka, who saw the light and became a peace-loving Buddhist well before the birth of Christ.(195) Gandhi himself used non-violence to extraordinary effect, as did another convert to the creed; Nelson Mandela. But these men have a modern advocate in an academic who has studied the ideology carefully and seen it put into practice to remarkable effect. The American Dr. Gene Sharp has written much on the potential of non-violence to topple violent regimes. He argues that to use violence against violence is self-defeating and usually pointless. Regime-change, he believes, is best achieved from inside but without the use of military aggression. Physical force and repression are the natural methods of brutal dictatorships. Use it and you will hand them a victory or at least the excuse to wage a protracted war against their own people. *"By placing confidence in violent means, one has chosen the very type of struggle with which the oppressors nearly always have superiority."* This is the cause of many an endless guerrilla war, with seldom a satisfactory outcome. This type of conflict, he argues, either maintains the existing power or simply replaces it with one of equal barbarity or in the words of Aristotle *"Tyranny can also change into tyranny."* In the 20th century, no one had a clearer understanding of this basic principle than Aldous Huxley; *". . . If any resistance is to be offered by the many to the few, it must be offered in a field in which technological superiority does not count . . . that (we) will be able to extort liberty from a ruling minority equipped by science with the very latest in self-propelled flame-throwers and atomic missiles seems in the highest degree unlikely. It is in satyagraha, or non-violent direct action, that the only hope of future revolutions resides."* And went on to say; *"The pen and the word are at least as mighty as the sword; for the sword is wielded in obedience to the spoken or written word."*(196)

In the 1990s, Dr Sharp was asked to write a handbook for those attempting to topple the military junta in Burma. As he declared himself unfamiliar with the complexities of Burmese politics, he wrote the book as a generic guide and called it *"From Dictatorship to Democracy."*(197) Sharp argued that all regimes rely on cooperation by a large section of the population and that if this were withdrawn in a variety of often subtle ways, the regime could not survive. He listed 198 'Methods' by which a regime could slowly but effectively be undermined. The book has since been translated into over 30 languages and far from a mere academic exercise, has been put into practice in many countries.

During the 2008/9 Iranian uprising the authorities accused the opposition parties of implementing 100 of his methods. Even in the recent uprising in Egypt, there is evidence that his book proved valuable to the anti-government protesters.(198)

Sharp's book is a brilliant tribute to the undeniable effectiveness of non-violence and its practical application. He focuses on the 'struggle' to 'disintegrate' regimes and replace them with 'democracy'. While he understands the many factors that can best topple autocracy and recognises the importance of internal over foreign action, he talks simply of the institution of democracy and only lightly of what he calls the *"intangible factors"* that make democracy work. He admits that there are *"intangible factors, psychological and ideological factors that may induce people to obey and assist the ruler."* But all we have come to understand in these pages has been about just these so-called intangible factors, not as vague unspecified notions but as the substance of faith and love that makes the world tick. For without the spiritual strength, or what is sometimes termed moral fibre and human dignity, democracy is a meaningless shell. It is the form without the content and as vulnerable to corruption as any human institution.

Sharpe also understood well that societies need the structures, whether guilds, societies or other institutions that underpin and separate workable authority in a country. But perhaps he understood less well the spirit that makes these institutions work judiciously. Ultimately and perhaps even unwittingly, he makes the case for passive resistance as an alternative to Britain declaring war on Nazi Germany in 1939. For he believes that if the structures and will exist, oppression can be resisted and overcome by non-violent means. If this is so and had Hitler invaded Britain, the occupying force could not have maintained control for long. There is no doubt that much suffering would have ensued but it probably would not have compared with the carnage and the long-term global trauma that actually occurred. No better proof of the wisdom of Gandhi's philosophy can be found than this clear realisation and its practical application today.

Again Gandhi hit the nail on the head when he addressed China following its invasion by Japan in 1937; *"You saying that your culture and morals are in danger of being destroyed, leads one to think that the reform movement in your country was only skin-deep . . . Blaming the wolf (Japan), would not help the sheep much. The sheep must learn not to fall into the clutches of the wolf."* (199) Gandhi truly believed that violence as a weapon against violence was not only futile but would prostitute the West to its nemesis and leave it vanquished; *"I suggest that at the end of the war, whichever way it ends, there will be no democracy left to represent democracy . . . It is a warning that if nobody reads the writing on the wall, man will be reduced to the state of the beast, whom he is shaming by his manners."* (200)

Change in Burma, believes the journalist Kate Adie; *"will have to come from inside"* (201). Aung San Suu Kyi understands perfectly the risks to democracy and its vulnerability. She realises that it is not the panacea in itself and that the West has paid a very high price for its violence. *"Freedom, democracy & human rights is not enough,"* she says, there must be a *"Revolution of the Spirit."* Democracy can become the slave of other 'dictatorships', those of commerce and the media, into which it can quietly slide. Daw Suu Kyi has repeatedly asked for action from the international communities to discredit the Burmese regime but despite diplomatic discussion, little has resulted of any substance. Similarly the Burma Campaign office in London, fighting for human rights in Burma, feels that the EU has made helpful noises but also failed to take any action that would put the regime under pressure. Anna Roberts, Executive Director of the BCUK stresses that such regimes do not function in isolation, indifferent to outside opinion. The military regime through their unelected party, the USDP, would not have put in place their *"Roadmap to Democracy"* or freed Daw Suu Kyi from house arrest, if they had not cared for world opinion.

If one assumes that peoples of the 'free world' care about freedom and the sufferings of those under repressive dictatorships, why have their elected representative made inadequate tangible moves to embarrass these regimes? In fact, as we have seen, the West has been happy to keep close relations - either in public or secret - and even promote ties with extremist governments. In every case commercial imperatives seem to come before all else in which the 'jugular' is invariably concern for fossil fuel supplies. It cannot be argued that these strategies reflect popular opinion and are therefore democratic when a Gallup poll taken in 2003, showed that eighty percent of Britons were against a second Iraq invasion, without sanction from the UN.(202) Why, except for the pursuit of oil, would the West choose regime change in Iraq, while so blatantly supporting other dictators across the globe? This can only point to a form of commercial dictatorship in the West, where violence and suffering are perpetrated against the will of the people.

Freedom in a democracy is essentially dependent on a free as well as varied media. Where the media is tied by political or commercial loyalties of any kind or threatened by the continual risk of monopoly, it cannot function effectively and democracy is fundamentally compromised. The word 'empire' when used to describe media giants such as News Corporation is not hyperbole. The power of nation states has to a great extent been replaced by that of virtual commercial empires, with trans global reach and without the traditional constraints. For example, the power of Rupert Murdoch to control and even dictate government policy in the United Kingdom has become strikingly overt in recent years. The British government relies heavily on media support and knows it could pay a lethal price for blocking the ambitions of such an 'empire'.(203)

So we have seen that democracy in name is no less vulnerable to corruption than any other institution or 'sacred cow'. What matters is the spirit or *intangible factors* that form its ideals and keep it true to its principles. Without them, so-called democratic nations can act as dictatorships, supporting extremism or even - as Gandhi pointed out - where power is so great, actually creating and perpetuating it. In these circumstances, dialogue, cooperation and integration is impossible and without these peace can never be the natural state of the world. The weakness of our institutions is the very reason why peace must come from each of us as individuals and why if Burma, Egypt or Libya are to find peace themselves, it must come from the collective hearts within each country. Gene Sharp highlighted the significance of these *intangible factors* in Poland in the 1980s and how, as an independent spiritual force, the Catholic Church had actually encouraged freedom in the fight against Communism. It is clear that without the spiritual dimension, if you like the 'will of the people' or the collective faith in the decency of humanity, no number of non-violent 'Methods' can actually advance a state towards democracy or for that matter maintain it there.

Hope for the world relies on every one of us recognising the difference between form and content and knowing when truth and love have left and movement is required to bring them back. This flexibility comes from a spiritual life, that is, one that concentrates on these very *intangible factors* and not the comforts of the material world, upon which we can never rely. This is exactly what Aung San Suu Kyi means by the need for a spirit revolution. And in this sentiment, she goes beyond Gene Sharp's 198 Methods. She has not spoken of *disintegration* for the Burmese regime, stating; *"I don't want to see the military fall but rise to new heights, I want them to be heroes."*(204) While she is obviously constrained by constant vigilance by the authorities, this statement is very much in keeping with her whole attitude to life as a Buddhist. When released from house arrest in 2010, she also stated; *". . I do not think that violence really pays - Violence begets more violence."*(205)

Gene Sharpe did understand the part such a spirit must play in the progress towards civilised governance. He touched on the spirit when in his book he used the words *"desire, strength & ability"* and *"determination, self-confidence & resistance skills."* But it is Aung San Suu Kyi who shows the way in which these qualities are realistically manifest. Her own inner peace means she can honestly say; *"I am for national understanding . . . I believe in human rights & the rule of law . . . I never hate another person or work for personal gain."*(206) She would not see herself as competing with anyone, whether individuals or group. With reference to her own political party, the NLD, she has said; *"We have to make sure that other parties are given the same rights as we are."* Regardless of the outside world, if the Buddhist and Christian communities are able to stand as one, with the spirit of non-violence and forgiveness, then it will be very difficult for any regime without a popular mandate to survive. And this is not an idle hope but a real possibility.

For further evidence of Daw Suu Kyi's spirit and intent beyond her own words one should consider the opinion of Alan Clements. As an American author and Buddhist who has studied Burma for 30 years, Clements traveled to Rangoon in 1995, met with Daw Suu Kyi in secret and recorded a series of dialogues with her that became the book *'Aung San Suu Kyi: The Voice of Hope'*. Clements is in no doubt about her intent; *"Aung San Suu Kyi is dedicated to the unification of all ethnicities and religious groups. Her revolution is one of the spirit and that means, as I understand her, including ALL aspects of the human heart and mind as natural to the whole. ALL beliefs. ALL persuasions. ALL religions. It also includes the many religious divisions within the military as well. She's a unifier. A healer. A builder of bridges. She does not harbor anger. Nor do her key colleagues. They are rooted in metta or loving-kindness."*(207) Representing a more mainstream British perspective, Benedict Rogers is Deputy Chairman of the Conservative Party Human Rights Commission and more specifically the Burmese representative for Christian Solidarity Worldwide. He completely concurs with the Buddhist Clements about Daw Suu Kyi's spirit; *"she is absolutely the one person who can unite everyone."*(208)

In a sense we've come full circle. If we change our own perspective, through a spiritual revolution, the equivalent of what Sharp called a *"powerful internal resistance force"*, the whole world around us must also change. The ability is within us if we choose to use it. So we need to look to our own house, inside ourselves and around our own community to change the world. We must see clearly the effects our attitudes and actions have had on the world. This is not just our good will but also our desire, ignorance and violence. The effects of our insatiable greed on the planet, ignorance of the needs of others and violence towards our fellow humans has denied us the peace that makes life bearable. But real peace must be more than absence of war, it must be a respect for the dignity of all humans and all creatures. Then nations will need no secrets or alliances, peace in the soul will make wars an irrelevance and we can all aim for whatever we choose to call it; Mettã; Moksha; Ataraxia or sublime union with God. In every language it is the mature spirit of dignity in which love can flourish and with it Peace.

"It has been an uplifting and recurring surprise to me that - whether you are trying to stop war, species extinction, starvation, pollution, resource destruction, or simply providing clean water for all - the solution only requires a change in our mind-set, replace; greed with self control, apathy with action, and disrespect with a gentle caring for everybody and everything" (209)

POSTSCRIPT

BACK DOWN THE STEPS OF PRAGMANISM

"Oh thanks be to God who allows me to tell of this
cruel agony that it should be known to the King.
You think by sowing death to plant for eternity?
. . . Oh King, beware that history does not say of you:
He was another Nero!
Is this the peace you give the world?
Such a gift awakens terror, profound horror!
The priest is a hangman, every soldier a bandit!
The people weep and die in silence,
your empire is a huge horrible dessert.
Like God the Redeemer, make the world whole anew,
soar to sublime heights above any other king!
Through you let the world rejoice! Grant it freedom!"

(From the Opera Don Carlos by Giuseppe Verdi)

So much theory is all very well but if these ideas are to carry any weight and stand up to the scrutiny of sceptics, it is important to see them at work in the real world. So let us turn our attention from the spirit alone, to its involvement in the world of 'realpolitik'. Suppose we have climbed the steps of 'enlightenment' to the top of the mountain and now must descend as Moses to the Israelites. We could take the particular example of Burma and its persistent non-violent struggle for democracy, as a litmus test of the theories we have considered. Then when tested satisfactorily, we can attempt to convey this spirit in material terms. That is to say, consider the ways these theories might be formulated into a simple creed to which we can easily relate and enact. But without wishing to reinvent the wheel, we can also judge examples of such creeds already in existence.

Despite the increased capacity for violence in mind and action facilitated by post-industrial development, taking the long view, there is a reassuringly positive outlook for humanity. Putting aside the admittedly appalling examples of violence witnessed in living memory, historians and others mindful of statistics tell us that levels of violence are generally diminishing in the world. Kate Allen, UK Director of Amnesty International, marked its 50th anniversary with the words; *"Fifty years on, we may well ask ourselves, 'What has changed?'. We may well sadly conclude, 'not a lot'. But that would be to underestimate the progress of the world in these past 50 years . . "*(210). The Dalai Lama is equally optimistic; *"There is a great and growing desire for change in the world; change that ushers in a renewed commitment to ethical and spiritual values, that resolves conflicts peaceably, employing dialogue and non-violence, that upholds human rights and human dignity as well as human responsibility."* (211)

Admittedly, immensely more efficient and varied forms of communication have brought graphic violence in a constant stream into our homes. This has undoubtedly produced a deceptive sense of increasing violence. But a detailed study of the subject has been made by the Harvard professor Steven Pinker, who claims, *"this is the most peaceful time in history."*(212) All forms of violence have apparently diminished. Certainly one can see that capital punishment is less frequent - itself an indicator of advancing societies - and other forms of sentencing generally less punitive. It is believed that while there are thought to have been around one hundred million violent deaths in the 20th Century, had the preceding trends been replicated and taking into account increased population, that number would have been more like two billion. The most significant reduction in levels of all violence began in the 18th century in the Northern European countries of Britain and The Netherlands. Many, including Pinker conclude that the Age of Enlightenment literally enlightened greater numbers of the population about the world around them.

This increased understanding, along with improvements in communication and literacy - assisted by technological advances - allowed for greater empathy. According to Pinker, as life became more valuable, people were worth more alive than dead. We have seen through the example of ancient Rome, how anyone outside the system was considered of no value and dispensable, often in a gruesome fashion for the cause of mass entertainment. Without any sense of association, it was easier to victimise outsiders. Humans as primates, function in groups, from families, friends, communities, to nations and other affiliations. Once, ignorance dictated that anyone beyond the immediate family was considered an alien and therefore if not a threat, without significance. Modern communications and education has seen the 'family of man' grow and with it, ever increasing amounts of global empathy and cooperation. This realisation is appreciated by the Dalai Lama when he says; "*Today we are so interdependent, so closely interconnected with each other, that without a sense of universal responsibility, a feeling of universal brotherhood and sisterhood, and an understanding and belief that we really are part of one big human family, we cannot hope to overcome the dangers to our very existence - let alone bring about peace and happiness.*" (213)

The countries associated with Western democracy can certainly be accused of diverging from the path of peace, especially in their 'imperialist' grasping for material gain. But considering the long-term perspective, the West can also be seen to have assisted the world's gradual progression towards peaceful coexistence. A good example of improving standards of civility can be found in the story of Aung San. As the father of Aung San Suu Kyi, he was the liberator of Burma from the British after the Second World War. In his desperation for allies, Aung San had sided with the Communists and then the Japanese but in 1945 he took the huge gamble - as a 'revolutionary criminal' - of returning to the British. He told the officer in command that he did not consider this move particularly risky. When asked why that was, he replied; *"Because you are a British officer."*(214) This is certainly not to deny the atrocities committed by any imperial or other power but simply to illustrate that beyond individual cases, one must consider the general trend. In 2004 Richard Lindley chaired a debate on the motion; *'The British Empire was a Force for Good'*. It brought together a worthy panel of Indian experts and while the motion was lost, even the most outspoken critics conceded that life was better under the British than any other comparable force.

That spirit of liberalism and greater understanding grew particularly in the newly formed Britain of the eighteenth century, in tandem with the Dutch tradition it inherited the previous century. This was a continuum fostered by various factors including the development of the Renaissance; the invention of the printing press; the culture of individualism fostered by the Reformation and of course, accelerating scientific progress. This spirit in turn took wing to the newly formed United States and is evident in the remarkably enlightened American Constitution. But even those fervent Englishman who forged this famous document, had not envisaged how their precious political system would gradually become irreparably factional. Early in the United States' history, there developed the basic split between left and right, between those that viewed themselves as 'liberal thinkers' and those who considered themselves experienced in the 'hard realities' of life. These two basic outlooks appear common to all political systems. In Friedrich Schiller's Play *'Don Carlos'*, the courtier Rodrigo implores King Philip II of Spain to see the horror perpetrated by him against the people of his vassal state. The drama is taken up in Verdi's libretto for the opera of the same name; *"Oh my lord, I have just come from Flanders, that land once so fair, now deprived of all light . . ."* Fortunately the king takes this criticism in the spirit intended but insists; *"By blood alone could I have peace in the world"* to which Rodrigo declares; *"La pace e dei sepolcri"* (it is the peace of the tomb). The king's response is perhaps predictably of the 'right' political inclination; *"Oh strange dreamer! You would change your ideas if you knew the heart of man as Philip knows it."* (215)

And so to Burma, where nearly fifty years have passed since the military coup under General Ne Win displaced democracy. It is also over twenty years since the first multi-party elections to follow that coup. The date was May 1990 and Aung San Suu Kyi won a landslide victory, though the Burmese government denied her power then and ever since. *"Has the campaign stalled?"* the BBC's John Simpson asked her in July 2011. The theory of non-violence and the spirit of Daw Suu Kyi cannot be faulted but there are now many voices declaring that the non-violent approach has proved ineffectual. Some critics would have greater militancy to effect change, while others disagree with the isolationist policy of sanctions and the restriction on tourism expounded by the NDL (National League for Democracy), of which she is the general secretary. Now there is an alternative democratic party gaining support. The National Democratic Front (NDF) - Burma is an acronymic minefield - encourages foreign involvement in Burma and has itself a military background. Founded in the 1970s, the movement has always had close links with the ethnic paramilitary groups fighting a guerrilla war with the Burmese regime (216). On its website, under 'Beliefs of the NDF', it states; *". . . Ethnic conflicts originating from political causes could only be resolved by political means and not by military means . . ."* But then seems to qualify that by adding somewhat ambiguously; *"the democratic forces must be organized for united struggle against the military regime."* (217)

Even those with obviously huge respect for Daw Suu Kyi, such as the writer Justin Wintle, appears to hint at some doubt in the NLD's approach; *"(Her) 'revolution of the spirit' seems to take the concept of revolution to a higher level . . . Whether it was the most appropriate package for a country as backward and authoritarian as Burma was, in 1990, is another matter."* If Pinker is right and the world is more peaceful because of greater integration and understanding, some say this is an argument in support of the alternative NDF's position of lifting sanctions and other international restrictions imposed on the regime. The face of politics becomes apparent in the assertion by the Burma Campaign UK that it is Western business interests that are backing the NDF's new approach, before any concern for the development of democracy in Burma. One can feel the pull of the 'right' against the quasi socialist, Buddhist, 'spirituality' personified by the NLD and Daw Suu Kyi. For Western business interests would claim free markets as the true arbiters of open 'free' society and herein lies the conundrum for Daw Suu Kyi. How democratic is this Western force at the gates of Rangoon and can 'The Lady' take on the whole world.

The truth is, Daw Suu Kyi's spiritual revolution recognises no ethnic or cultural bounds. It is as much aimed at violence tolerated in the name of democracy, as under any totalitarian regime. This is the reason why her cause and dogged determination has won her so much support in the West. When Justin Wintle speaks of her taking her 'revolution of the spirit' to a higher level, he sites this as; *"one reason why she is admired in actual democracies where secularist materialism may create a vacuum of the spirit."* It is an essential part of the spirituality of Daw Suu Kyi that she does not allow herself dogmatic statements that fail to see the bigger picture. In attacking a particular Burmese leader or political system, one risks missing the spirit behind it. This is why she called not for the fall of the regime, to be merely replaced by another similar, but for the leaders *"to be heroes."* For the same reason, she does not condemn the institution of the military itself, of which in Burma, her father was once the commander, any more than Jesus would have in Roman times. For, as we have seen, it is the ability of the spiritually aware to look beyond mere form to the meaning and motivation beyond. Ever seeing the potential rather than the abuse, she views the army as *"a force of protection rather than a force of destruction . . . one could say that to maintain a professional, honourable, army would be an act of common sense."*(218)

But is Daw Suu Kyi naive, as many on the right of politics imply? The BBC's John Simpson, who was the first to talk with her after her release from house arrest in November 2010, is as good a voice to turn to as any. As the BBC's World Affairs Editor for over twenty years, Simpson has witnessed the world from the sharp end. This is a man who travelled back from Paris to Tehran with the exiled Ayatollah Khomeini in 1979 and has never been far from the action in every volatile part of the globe since. Perhaps his courteous meeting with Daw Suu Kyi that November had required hiding his true feeling I asked him. Not at all he replied; *"I admire her hugely."* But was she misguided? *"She is an exemplary individual and I utterly agree with her non-violent principles . . . She know exactly what she is doing and progress is being made."* But then he went on; *"I definitely support the approach of the NLD . . . Daw Suu Kyi is an idealist but definitely not naive . . . Though it is all very well for me to sit here and say so, real progress in Burma means action (non-violent) and as Daw Suu Kyi has said herself, it needs commitment and bravery. Though it is tough to say so, martyrs really help. Nelson Mandela and Daw Suu Kyi are very much 'martyrs' to their causes. Burma needs more action and yes, Gene Sharp's 198 Methods would be very useful. The 'Madres de Plaza de Mayo' made a real difference through their suffering and changed Argentina. Look at South America now, what a huge move forward towards civilisation."* Simpson also agrees the world is becoming a better place, however slow that progress towards universal consensus politics. Dictators, he senses, are becoming harder to find and even the Burmese regime finds in necessary to talk of democracy; *"Burma's 'Roadmap to Democracy' was a very good sign of this . . . Violence in the world is in its death throes."* In fact a friend high up in the government of China, had recently said to him that these days; *"you don't know how insecure a government feels that is unelected."*(219)

Justin Wintle has made an in-depth study of Burma and the cause of democracy there. While he has remained dispassionate about the moving story of General Aung San's daughter, he is in no doubt about her significance and that of the non-violent movement today. *"The cornerstone of Suu Kyi's emerging Buddhism was Matta, loving-kindness or empathic care to all sentient beings."* The bedrock of her strength was the Buddhist 'Vipassana' method: *"mental concentration through controlled, conscious breathing,"* as we observed in Step 2. *"Meditation has helped to strengthen me spiritually in order to follow the right path"* she has said. *"Also for me, meditation is part of a way of life because what you do when you meditate is to learn to control your mind through developing awareness. This awareness carries on into everyday life. For me, that's one of the most practical benefits of meditation - my sense of awareness has become heightened. I'm now much less likely to do things carelessly and unconsciously."*(220) According to Wintle; *"Suu Kyi's position was that to resort to force of any kind, however physically inconsequential, would fatally damage the principles she stood for. Any victory gained by violence would only perpetuate violence, and it was Burma's historic culture of violence that she wished to dismantle. If the Tatmadaw* (the Burmese military) *wanted to confront her, then she would meet them face-to-face, unarmed and undefended."* For Daw Suu Kyi; 'freedom from fear' was intended as much for the regime itself as anyone else, being the *"fear of losing power."* The use of violence; *"only institutionalises violence."* This she made plain in what she called the *'Animal Farm syndrome',* where a new regime could replicate the worst aspects of the previous. *"A revolution which aims merely at changing official policies and institutions with a view to an improvement in material conditions has little chance of genuine success. Without a revolution of the spirit, the forces that produced the iniquities of the old order would continue to be operative, posing a constant threat to the process of reform and regeneration."*

To study her background is to appreciate that Daw Suu Kyi in no light-weight in understanding the complexities of politics. Her life and studies had taken her to India, while her mother was ambassador; Britain to study PPE at Oxford; the United States as a researcher for the United Nations and to Japan for further study. Her beliefs therefore are grounded in a broad understanding and combine the principles of Buddhism; the non-violence of Gandhi; the precepts of the UN; as well as Anglo-Saxon liberalism. And yet she did not consider democracy the end in itself, for Daw Suu Kyi has always had the understanding to look beyond the label alone. In the words of Wintle, she believed; *"the principles of liberal democracy are already embedded in Burmese history"*, with *"democracy and Buddhism (the bedrock of Burmese culture), wholly compatible."* She is evidently talking of the 'spirit' of democracy here over an institution championed by the 'Free World'. In fact she has expressed reservations about the spirit of violence that she sees pervading the West. Once asked what concerned her most about Western democracy, she replied; *"It all comes down to violence. The kind of songs and music and films . . . deal with violence in some form or other."*(221) As an individual seen by many as contributing hugely to the *'Confraternity of mankind',* it is no wonder that in 1991 she was awarded a Nobel Prize for Peace.

That broad understanding of the ways of humanity has also helped her see the bigger, long-term picture. Even if by necessity, it requiring more time to grow to full maturity, she recognises the spirit that must triumph. *"When I despair,"* wrote Mohandas Gandhi *"I remember that all through history, the way of truth and love have always won. There have been tyrants and murderers, and for a time they can seem invincible, but in the end they always fall. Think of it - always."*(222) So, in the light of mounting pressure for greater signs of progress towards democracy in Burma, Has the campaign stalled? Without faltering Daw Suu Kyi replies; *"there's never just one way in politics."* *"Rather than force a showdown with the regime"* Simpson observed *"she'd prefer to take the long road."*(223)

In contrast to Simpson, Alan Clements was the first American to be ordained as a Buddhist monk in Burma and spent six months in discussion with Daw Suu Kyi about her life and beliefs. If one assumes that no one understands the spirit she exemplifies better, it is to the erudite Clements we should now turn for final clarification. To the question is she naive, he replies; *"Absolutely not! She is a 'super pragmatist'. One should never underestimate what this woman is achieving in these complicated circumstances . . . understanding the value of freedom for the long-term (she) embodies proactive love, 'I respect you and see beyond your fear.'"* But Clements understands the risk of seeing her as more than simply a vehicle for a greater concept, a notion she would herself abhor. He continues; *"I'm a fan of her values not her person, she is a metaphor for a non-local language beyond ethnicity and a great heroine of universal freedom but freedom is larger than Suu Kyi, a leader of universal revolution. The genie is out of the bottle. She doesn't need to leave Burma to travel the world."*(224) From a powerful advocate, this is a clear statement of the *'Revolution of the Spirit'*, so fundamental to Daw Suu Kyi's belief system; so ancient and yet, gradually gaining credibility worldwide. Clements summarises it as *"radical self reliance and self development"* adding; *"this far exceeds what King (M.L.) and Gandhi did - to engender an understanding of 'hiri' (moral shame) - on the outside and 'ottappa' (moral regret) on the inside."*

Of course, in considering the case of Burma - now renamed 'The Republic of the Union of Myanmar' by its military regime - we must tread gentle in an extremely complex situation. There are no simple solutions and the causes and effects of the Burmese situation are not always immediately apparent. If we are considering the practical application of non-violence, we must bear in mind its varying interpretations and implications. In her second Reith Lecture in 2011, Daw Suu Kyi spoke of adopting non-violence; *"not on moral grounds, as some believe. Only on practical political grounds."* (225). One wonders what Mohandas Gandhi would have made of this declaration, perhaps considering a 'Revolution of the Spirit' to have a moral imperative as its very raison d'etre. Deep in the Burmese psyche is the notion that the Tatmadaw 'liberated' the country from British domination and was instrumental, through her father General Aung San, in providing for democracy. Great respect for her father and a deep-rooted national equation of the Tatmadaw with stability and former royal glory, may be colouring perspectives here. It could also be subconsciously giving validity to the notion of change by violent means. However, most historians argue it was the debilitating outcome of the Second World War on Britain, an anti-imperialist Labour government coming to power with an end to the Indian Empire, that were the crucial factors in Burma achieving independence. (226) Important though these events were, the British would have been very aware that it was the overwhelming and possibly insurmountable 'will' of the various Burmese peoples that made independence a real inevitability. It is likely that Gene Sharp would agree with this as well as Gandhi. Non-violence isn't just a practicality; it is an essential prerequisite to mature progress towards peace in the world.

So for a clearer understanding of Gandhi's perspective on non-violence, one can turn to the analysis of Dr. Ramin Jahanbegloo; *" . . Gandhi's message lays the foundation for a renewed vision of nonviolence as an antidote to terrorism and unilateral politics in our world. . . According to Gandhi, the greatest moral duty was to fight the unjust even though it may cause us to suffer, because through our suffering we can show others the mistake they are* *making. Gandhi knew that violence unlike anger is not a natural phenomenon and it ultimately robs us of our humanity. Therefore he invited us to change our life style and our way of looking at things in order to be able to change the world. He said: "You must be the change you want to see in the world." The power of these words, spoken over 60 years ago, is often drowned out in the social and political violence of today's world. But Gandhi is probably the most important thinker whose precepts could guide the crisis-ridden world of 21st century . . "* (227)

2007 was the year of 'non-violent' civil unrest in Burma, involving thousands of Buddhist monks, which came to be known as the 'Saffron Revolution'. Almost exactly a year later (and incidentally, two and a half years before the Nato air strikes commenced over Libya), the leader of the British opposition party, David Cameron declared; *"We should accept that we cannot impose democracy at the barrel of a gun; that we cannot drop democracy from 10,000 feet and we shouldn't try."*(228) Of course he was right to say it, democracy is change by consensus not force. John Simpson agrees with Manningham-Buller that democracy can't be forged with military force, adding; *"Ireland wasn't winnable in a military sense . . . nor, even, was the emergency in Malaya. It is often necessary to counter force with force at first, but politics and diplomacy always have to come in as quickly as they can be deployed."* In fact he believes that violent action actually delays the progress towards eventual democratic rule; *"Ireland is only one example, but it's probably the best one. South Africa is another; an entirely peaceful campaign by the ANC would I think have brought about a solution quicker."* We should concede and most will agree that there are instances when force is required and where military power is a necessary 'evil'; in the words of Kate Adie; *"A hammer is sometimes required to pry dictator's fingers off the window ledge of power"* (229). What we have learned however, is that it cannot win the long-term peace and that this may only be achieved through non-military, peaceful engagement. In the words of Ben Ferencz, Chief Prosecutor for the US at the Nuremberg Tribunal in 1945; *"I have learned that you cannot kill an ideology with a gun; vengeance begets more vengeance."*(230) Lasting peace can only be accomplished with understanding, cooperation and compromise.

So democracy is the civil enactment of the spirit of understanding and respect, resulting from individual actions of love. Not only have we seen a steady move towards less violence in the world but according to the most observant, the trend is matched by a gradual, greater participation in and understanding of democracy worldwide. Simpson is not alone in believing multilateral peace a realistic goal for the world and he does not think it at all fanciful to look to an age when nations will no longer need secrets and alliances. *"When you think how fast the world has moved to multilateralism, and extend the graph onwards into the future, you can see how the old systems could well die out. The obvious examples are France and Germany, but there are so many others. Already, countries which think in purely self-centred ways seem a little old-fashioned."*(231)

So an individual recognises the spirit of love and by subtle adjustment climbs the steps of awareness and is transformed. Where we go, others will follow and an enlightened conscience is manifest in many enhancing actions. By exponential increments, are the steps then descended to realism in a world we can change for the better. That world is our home and our sanity in the end relies on the world's long-term sanity. It will apparently get there on its own but we have the power to help it, an extraordinary power to improve our lives and those around us. We can smooth the progress not just through our families or friends, not just our immediate communities but beyond, to the outside world and all 'sentient beings'. In the end, by expression of our true maturity, we fear nothing and reach out in love to all and in so doing, understand that fear is merely ignorance and loving-kindness heals all.

The genie is indeed out of the bottle . . .

"You are free. You are free to go to your temples. You are free to go to your mosques or to any other places of worship in this state of Pakistan. You may belong to any religion, caste or creed – that has nothing to do with the business of the State. We are starting with this fundamental principle, that we are all citizens and citizens of one state"

PAKISTAN'S FOUNDER - MOHAMMED ALI JINNAH (1947)

THE CHARTERS

Through the pages of this book we have come to appreciate that no word or action can truly represent a spirit, which is by definition non-material and if you like, the 'content with no lasting form'. We have also seen the formulation of an understanding of what it is to be truly 'mature' and precisely because it is a spirit, it is unrelated to a person's age, status or education. Therefore, intended as no more than an helpful reminder, I offer below a simple guide and have called it **'The Chandos Charter'**.

We can rest assured that the 'form' to which we can apply our clearer sense of 'spirit' already exists. It is enshrined in various documents such as the United Nation's **'Declaration of Human Rights'**, the preamble from which is included here. There are many others such as the *'Millennium Development Goals'* and the *'Kyoto Protocol'* (for the environment). But it will require the will; the spirit of sufficient numbers to reach the tipping point towards real progress.

The essence of this form and spirit are no better synthesised than in the *'Call for Action'* of Rights and Humanity, the NGO founded by Professor Julia Hausermann and blazing a trail towards a new understanding for a better world. You can read *'Shining the Light - A Call for Action'* and spread the 'spirit' by becoming a signatory at;

www.rightsandhumanityglc.org

"The time for the lone wolf is over.
Gather yourselves!
Banish the word struggle from your attitude and your vocabulary.
All that we do now must be done in a sacred manner
and in celebration.
We are the ones we've been waiting for..." (232)

THE CHANDOS CHARTER

We have learned that there are certain constant and universal standards that characterise truly civilised society.

And we assert that for humanity:

1) **Dignity** means being reflective, a good listener and having appropriate restraint

2) **Respect** is the natural entitlement of all; particularly those we do not understand and we cherish the differences between people, working always for the good of others

3) **We do not hate or create enemies,** recognising hatred as an emotion of ignorance and fear, working always towards peaceful resolutions

4) **Tolerance** is as important as the constant need for dialogue with those with whom we disagree

5) **Forgiveness** is imperative for any offence and while the law will judge, we are not judgmental and therefore we seek no revenge

6) **Courage** overcomes many limitations and we accept the need for constant change in the world, so that we are always open to new possibilities and good advice

7) **Limits are recognised,** where we are powerless over so much in life, realistic about the world and at times vulnerable, renouncing our desire to control others

8) **Ego is a stumbling block,** trust all-important and the ways of nature our guiding principle

9) **Sacrifice, endurance and self-discipline** are entirely natural and freely applied and with understanding, allow us to act rather than simply react

10) **Humour** and laughter bring joy and sanity to the world

---

**If you have enjoyed reading this book
and agree with the principles of the Chandos Charter,
you can join us by becoming a signatory:**

www.evolvingthespirit.com

THE UNIVERSAL DECLARATION OF HUMAN RIGHTS

PREAMBLE

WE THE PEOPLES OF THE UNITED NATIONS DETERMINED

- to save succeeding generations from the scourge of war, which twice in our lifetime has brought untold sorrow to mankind, and

- to reaffirm faith in fundamental human rights, in the dignity and worth of the human person, in the equal rights of men and women and of nations large and small, and

- to establish conditions under which justice and respect for the obligations arising from treaties and other sources of international law can be maintained, and

- to promote social progress and better standards of life in larger freedom,

AND FOR THESE ENDS

- to practice tolerance and live together in peace with one another as good neighbours, and

- to unite our strength to maintain international peace and security, and

- to ensure, by the acceptance of principles and the institution of methods, that armed force shall not be used, save in the common interest, and

- to employ international machinery for the promotion of the economic and social advancement of all peoples,

HAVE RESOLVED TO COMBINE OUR EFFORTS TO ACCOMPLISH THESE AIMS

Accordingly, our respective Governments, through representatives assembled in the city of San Francisco, who have exhibited their full powers found to be in good and due form, have agreed to the present Charter of the United Nations and do hereby establish an international organization to be known as the United Nations.

Article 2

3) All Members shall settle their international disputes by peaceful means in such a manner that international peace and security, and justice, are not endangered.

4) All Members shall refrain in their international relations from the threat or use of force against the territorial integrity or political independence of any state, or in any other manner inconsistent with the Purposes of the United Nations.

ACKNOWLEDGEMENTS

The glossary of quotes that follows, gives testament of the vast array of wisdom that has supported me in my writing. From ancient greats to modern inspiration, I give thanks for the strength drawn from them. I am particularly grateful for the many who have discussed the issues and given me the benefit of their expert advice. Many are listed in the glossary. But for their particular kindness and consideration, I should give a special mention to Anna Roberts, Alan Clements, John Simpson, Kate Adie, Ben Rogers, Roger Royle, Tamsin Mitchell, Roger Wisdom, Sir John & Lady Tavener, George Tomlin, Eve Branson and David Holzer. Jennifer Coombs has proved a tireless ally in rallying support from some impressive friends, as have equally Lord and Lady Digby.

I am grateful for the time and measured advise given by Chowdhury Mueen-Uddin, a founder of the Muslim Council of Britain and Reverend Zeev Amit representing the United Synagogues. I am also grateful for the advice given by the Foreign Secretary, William Hague and generous support from the Secretary of State for the Cabinet Office, Oliver Letwin. Their willingness to support my research surely gives hope for an open society.

I am also indebted for their help to the many founders of like-minded organisations and I should particularly mention; Jane Ozanne, Anna Lubelska, Professor Julia Hausermann, Juliet Rogers, Sue Hale and Inge Relph.

I particularly want to acknowledge the influence of my family, who's loving support and advice has been as a backbone for further development and inquiry. My mother Doreen Gildea was my constant sounding board and eagle eye and my stepmother (whom my mother would not object to my calling a second mother) Pamela Russell has been equally encouraging and hugely supportive. My half-brother James Russell (otherwise known as the monk Kaliyaphani) was my authority on Hinduism. Gratitude to my family would not be complete without acknowledging the impact of my father. Rodney Russell was a gentle, kind and thoughtful man, who's paintings spoke only of peace, while his poetry moved many. His disciplined, loving life was an inspiration for so many beside myself, and this book was easier to write because of him.

Last and most certainly not least, I gratefully recognise the love and support of my partner Sean Wong, without whose good sense and endless patience, this endeavour would have been impossible.

> *". . . a sufficiency of non-violent heat*
> *will melt the hardest heart"* (233)

SOME FURTHER READING

AN INTEGRAL VISION - Ken Wilber

BURMA, WHAT EVERYONE NEEDS TO KNOW - David I Steinberg

FROM DICTATORSHIPTO DEMOCRACY - Gene Sharp

PEACE IS POSSIBLE - Fredrik S Heffermehl

PERFECT HOSTAGE - Justin Wintle

SACRED IS THE DUST - Rodney F Russell

SCIENCE, LIBERTY & PEACE - Aldous Huxley

SMALL IS BEAUTUFUL - E F Schumaker

THAN SHWE, UNMASKING BURMA'S TYRANT - Benedict Rogers

THE ART OF LOVING - Erich Fromm

THE LADY AND THE PEACOCK - Peter Popham

THE PROPHET - Kahil Gibran

THE TAO OF PHYSICS - Fritjof Capra

THE VOICE OF HOPE - Alan Clements

TO HAVE OR TO BE? - Erich Fromm

UNRELIABLE SOURCES - John Simpson

WAR AND PEACE - Leo Tolstoy

WAR PLAN IRAQ - Milan Rai

WHAT DOES GANDHI WANT? - T A Raman

WITH GRATEFUL THANKS

Amnesty International - www.amnesty.org.uk

Burma Campaign UK - www.burmacampaign.org.uk

Christian Solidarity Worldwide - www.csw.org.uk

Dreamstar Books - www.dreamstarbooks.com

Muslim Council of Britain - www.mcb.org.uk

Peter Tatchell Foundation - www.petertatchellfoundation.org

Revolution of the Spirit - www.revolutionofthespirit.com

Rights and Humanity - www.rightsandhumanity.org

Shepheard Walwyn - www.ethicaleconomics.org.uk

Spirit of Peace - www.spiritofpeace.co.uk

Spiritual England - www.spiritualengland.org.uk

Support for the Oppressed Peoples of Burma - www.sopb.org

Tamsin Mitchell - www.tamsinmitchell.co.uk

United Synagogue - www.theus.org.uk

World Dharma - www.worlddharma.com

Anthony Russell

Educated in Spain and at Bryanston School and reading Art History at Oxford Brookes, Anthony Russell worked as a fine art auctioneer and antique dealer in London before moving back to the West Country to follow the family tradition as a professional artist.

Travelling extensively around the world, he combined painting with tour lecturing, principally to American university students on bespoke tours of Europe.

He spent six years as a consultant for Luke Hughes and toured the country advising prestigious buildings on their furniture needs, including museums, palaces, schools and cathedrals. Now based in London, he spends much of his time lecturing and undertaking research, while helping at the British Museum, hosting outreach events and visiting lecturers. His own lecture program includes presentations to the Church of England, architects, national and local societies and charities.

He has published various articles on architecture and spirituality and contributed to 'The Ultimate Australian Adventure Guide'. He is passionate about the importance of art and music and their role in promoting 'understanding, cooperation and integration', which prompted him to found 'The Chandos'. He has helped run a therapeutic community in Dorset and spent extended periods in Zimbabwe and Argentina, undertaking research. This book is inspired by a life-long commitment to the principles of non-violence and is intended as recognition of its brave standard-bearers through history.

www.thechandos.com

GLOSSARY

of quotes and references

(a) - *"Lord, make me an instrument of your peace . . "* The prayer was submitted anonymously to a small French spiritual magazine called *La Clochette* (The Little Bell) in 1912, and although the author has never been firmly established, it is known as the Prayer of Saint Francis, having been found in Normandy in 1915, written on the back of a holy card of St. Francis of Assisi.

A DESERT CALLED PEACE

(b) - *"They rob, kill & rape and call this 'Roman Rule'. They create a desert called 'Peace'"* The Celtic leader Calgacus, (fought against the Roman general Agricula in northern Scotland), quoted by the senator & Roman historian **Tacitus** (AD 56 – AD 117) in his book 'Agricula'

BACKCLOTH

(1) - *"Modern physics has shown that the rhythm of creation and destruction is not only manifest in the turn of the seasons and in the birth and death of all living creatures, but is also the very essence of inorganic matter,"* and that *"For the modern physicists, then, Shiva's dance is the dance of subatomic matter."* **Fritjof Capra** (b. 1939) From his book 'The Tao of Physics' (1975)

(2) - *"Where wealth accumulates and men decay"* (1769). **Oliver Goldsmith** (1730-1774)

PREFACE

(3) - *"We do not need to proselytise either by our speech or by our writing. We can only do so really with our lives. Let our lives be open books for all to study".* **Mohandas Gandhi** (1869-1948)

(4) - *"All know the way, but few actually walk it."* **The Bodhidharma** (5th/6th century Buddhist monk)

(5) - **Kōbō-Daishi** (774-835AD) Father of Japan's Shingon Sect. In 830 Kukai completed his systematization of Shingon doctrines in his *Jujushinron* (Ten Stages of Mind Development).

(6) - *"Self-evident".* American Constitution (1776): *"We hold these truths to be self-evident, that all men are created equal . . . "*

(7) - *". . as soon as you remove the cobwebs of ignorance that surround it, (the truth) shines clear"* **Mohandas Gandhi** (1869-1948)

(8) - *"The best system we have",* **Sir Winston Churchill** (1874-1965). The real quote: *" . . No one pretends that democracy is perfect or all-wise. Indeed, it has been said that democracy is the worst form of government except all those other forms that have been tried from time to time . . "* (1947)

(9) - *"Market Failure".* See Wikipedia: http://en.wikipedia.org/wiki/Economics#Market_failure.

(10) - *". . . if economic thinking pervades the whole of society, even simple non economic values like beauty, health or cleanliness can survive only if they prove to be 'economic'".* From the book "Small is Beautiful" by **E F Schumacher** (1911- 1977)

(11) - 'Nirvana' - is the Buddhist state of perfect peace reached by not wanting more than you have. It means happiness and peace. It is every Buddhist's goal to achieve Nirvana. The **Buddha** described it as: *"the far shore, the subtle, the very difficult to see, the unaging, the stable, the undisintegrating, the unmanifest, the unproliferated, the peaceful, the deathless , the sublime, the auspicious, the secure, the destruction of craving, the wonderful, the amazing, the unailing, the unailing state, the unafflicted, dispassion, purity, freedom, the unadhesive, the island, the shelter, the asylum, the refuge..."*

(12) - 'The Minnesota Method'. Based on the 12 Step model of the fellowship of Alcoholics Anonymous (AA)

(13) - *"Do as I say, not as I do"*. **John Selden** (1584-1654). An English Jurist & philosopher, from *Table-Talk* (c. 1654): *"Preachers say, 'Do as I say, not as I do.'"*

(14) - *"People today are yearning for human beings who have wisdom and conviction and the courage to act according to their convictions."* From 'To Have or to Be?' (1976), book by **Erich Fromm** (1900-1980) - humanistic philosopher

STEP 1 - THE GAP

(15) - *"Where there is nothing, there is God."* **St Augustine** (354-430) or **W.B.Yeats** (1865-1939): *"we shall not come to that joy, that battle, till we have put out the senses, everything that can be seen and handled, as I put out this candle. [He puts out candle.] We must put out the whole world as I put out this candle [puts out another candle]. We must put out the light of the stars and the light of the sun and the light of the moon [puts out the rest of the candles], till we have brought everything to nothing once again. I saw in a broken vision, but now all is clear to me. Where there is nothing, where there is nothing - there is God!"* Plays 381 The Unicorn from the Stars (1908)

(16) - **William James** (1842-1910) was a pioneering American psychologist and philosopher who trained as a medical doctor. He wrote influential books on the young science of psychology and was the bother of Henry James. 'Penicillin'; The antibiotic properties of Penicillium fungi were discovered (1928), by the Scottish scientist and Nobel laureate **Alexander Fleming** (1881-1955), for the groundbreaking treatment of bacterial infections such as syphilis and staphylococcus.

"But if the religion of exclusive scientificism should ever succeed in suffocating all other appetites out of a nation's mind, and imbuing a whole race with the persuasion that simplicity and consistency demand a 'tabula rasa' to be made of every notion that does not form part of the 'soi-disant' scientific synthesis, that nation, that race, will just as surely go to ruin, and fall a prey to their more richly constituted neighbors, as the beasts of the field, as a whole, have fallen a prey to man." From the essay 'Reflex, action & Theism'

by **William James** (an address delivered to the Unitarian Ministers' Institute at Princeton, Mass., 1881, and printed in the 'Unitarian Review' for October of that year)

(17) - Information from article by **Richard Levins** (b. 1930), awarded the 1996 Edinburgh Medal (Edinburgh International Science Festival); *" . . . But science also has had dramatic failures. The promises of understanding and progress have not been kept, and the application of science to human affairs has often done great harm. Public health institutions were caught by surprise by the resurgence of old diseases and the appearance of new ones. Modern planning has not given us more habitable cities. Industrial design for greater efficiency has not made work more humane but, instead, led to increased bodily stress, anxiety, overwork and unemployment. Pesticides increase pests, create new pest problems and contribute to the load of poison in our habitat. Antibiotics create new pathogens resistant to our drugs. Modern high-tech agronomy watches our soils disappearing. The green revolution did not eliminate hunger but increased the polarisation between rich and poor and the dependence of developing countries on imports. Scientific theories have even been put forth to justify inequality, racism, aggression and competitiveness . . . "*

(18) - *"Life is a mystery to be lived not a problem to be solved"*. Author unknown. Alternatively: *"Imagination is more important than knowledge"*. **Albert Einstein** (1879-1955)

(19) - *"Science may set limits to knowledge, but should not set limits to imagination."* **Bertrand Russell** (1872 - 1970). British philosopher, mathematician and social commentator

(20) - Most Dutch 17th century painting presented a rich tapestry of meaning, with many objects bearing symbolic meaning. " *. . very many Dutch paintings . . filter the perception of the eye through the lens of moral sensibility"*. **Simon Schama** (b. 1945) in the introduction to his book 'The Embarrassment of Riches' (1991)

(21) - *"Petty private beliefs"*. **Professor Richard Dawkins** (b. 1941). From 'The Genius of Charles Darwin' (Channel 4 UK TV 2009)

(22) - *"but I'm not interested in substance, it's the essence of the music that counts!"* **Sir John Tavener** (b. 1948). British composer, best known for 'Song of Athene', played at the funeral of Princess Diana (1997)

(23)   *"we fall"*. King James Holy Bible, Proverbs 16:18 warns: *"Pride goeth before destruction, and a haughty spirit before a fall."*

(24) - *"Nature abhors a vacuum"*. **Francois Rabelais** (1493 - 1553)

(25) - *'To Have or to Be?'* (1976). Book by **Erich Fromm** (1900-1980) the humanist philosopher.

(26) - 'The Selfish Gene' (1976). Book by **Professor Richard** Dawkins (b. 1941). In his foreword to the 30th edition, Dawkins admitted he could *"readily see that [the book's title] might give an inadequate impression of its contents"* and that in retrospect it might better have been entitled *'The Immortal Gene.'*

(27) - *"What the sources of property are does not matter; nor does possession impose any obligations on the property owner. The principle is: 'Where and how my property was acquired or what I do with it is nobody's business but my own; as long as I do not violate the law, my right is unrestricted and absolute."* **Erich Fromm** (1900-1980). From the book 'To Have or to Be?' (1976)

(28) - *"To maintain control over private property we need to use power to protect it from those who would take it from us, because they, like us, can never have enough; the desire to have private property produces the desire to use violence . . "* **Erich Fromm** (1900-1980). From the book 'To Have or to Be?'

(29) - *"Economy as a content of life is a deadly illness, because infinite growth does not fit into a finite world. That economy should not be the content of life has been told to mankind by all the great teachers"*. **E F Schumacher** (1911-1977) Economist

(30) - *"It is obvious to everybody that we are in a process of cultural self destruction. What is left is not secure any more"*. *"For two or three centuries many individuals have lived only as working beings and not as human beings."* **Albert Schweitzer** (1875-1965) theologian & philosopher

(31) - *" . . . until the conquest (of nature) has become more and more equivalent to destruction. Our sprit of conquest and hostility has blinded us to the fact that natural resources have their limit and can eventually be exhausted, and that nature will fight back against human rapaciousness."* **Erich Fromm** (1900-1980). From the book 'To Have or To Be?' (1976)

(32) - *"We need to find God, and he cannot be found in noise and restlessness. God is the friend of silence. See how nature - trees, flowers, grass- grows in silence; see the stars, the moon and the sun, how they move in silence... We need silence to be able to touch souls."* **Mother Teresa** (1910-1997)

STEP 2 - BREATHING

(33) - *"Whenever I feel blue, I start breathing again".* **Lyman Frank Baum** (1856-1919). American author of children's books, best known for writing *'The Wonderful Wizard of Oz'* (1900)

(34) - Cure for hiccups. The theory of **Rodney F Russell** (1918-1995), painter and poet & father of the author

(35) - 'Existential Angst'. Literally anxiety about one's existence. From the philosophical movement Existentialism, started in the 19th century. *"Existentialist - a philosopher who emphasizes freedom of choice and personal responsibility but who regards human existence hostile universe as unexplainable."* (wordnetweb.princeton.edu/perl/webwn) Angst is the dread coming from experience of human freedom & responsibility.

(36) - *". . . sleep is the only proper situation for inactivity, the state of awakeness is one in which laziness should have no place"* *"The paradoxical situation with a vast number of people today, is that they are half asleep when awake and half awake when asleep or when they want to sleep."* **Erich Fromm** (1900-1980) from the book 'The Art of Loving.' A German American, Jewish humanist philosopher & Marxist.

(37) - *"In love's godlike breathing, there's the innermost aspect of the universe".* **Alexander Scriabin** (1872-1915) Russian composer & pianist

STEP 3 - LISTENING

(38) - *"Beyond the spectrum is what we do not see."* The vast majority of the electromagnetic spectrum is invisible. The highest frequencies

known are gamma rays, x-rays and ultraviolet light, while the lower frequencies of the spectrum are Infrared radiation, microwaves and radio waves. Visible light falls within a very narrow range in between

(39) - 'Grave-en.' Grave = *"any place that becomes the receptacle of what is dead, lost, or past: the grave of unfulfilled ambitions"* En = *to make verb from the noun (Dictionary.com)*

(40) - *"If one is after quick results, one never learns an art. Yet, for modern man, patience is as difficult to practice as discipline and concentration."* From '*The Art of Loving*' (1956) by **Erich Fromm** (1900-1980)

(41) - *"Sometimes one creates a dynamic impression by saying something, and sometimes one creates as significant an impression by remaining silent."* **The Dalai Lama** (b. 1935)

(42) - '*Intercede*' - inter-cede. From the Latin: *Inter* (among, in the midst of, together) and *cede* (yield, to go).

(43) - *"God is love"* **St Paul the Evangelist**, *"Whoever does not love does not know God, because God is love."* 1 John 4:8 (New International Version of the Bible)

(44) - *"God reveals Himself through his 'theophanies', whether it be through Christ, the Buddha, or virgin nature or in the word made book, The Koran. Gods shows himself in everything that lives and this includes the sublime language of music."* **Sir John Tavener** (b. 1944), British composer & visionary

(45) *"humanity needs all the world's religions to suit the ways of life, diverse spiritual needs, and inherited national traditions of individual human beings."* And he goes further; *"every major religion of the world - Buddhism, Christianity, Confucianism, Hinduism, Islam, Jainism, Judaism, Sikhism, Taoism, Zoroastrianism - has similar ideals of love, the same goal of benefiting humanity through spiritual practice, and the same effect of making their followers into better human beings."* **The Dalai Lama** (b.1935), 'A Human Approach to Peace' from 'Massages' on his website; www.thedalailama.com

(46) - *"You talk when you cease to be at peace with your thoughts."* From 'The Prophet' by **Kahlil Gibran** (1883-1931). Lebanese American poet & writer.

(47) - *"We cannot burst other people's bubbles, only our own"*. The psychotherapist **Tamsin Mitchell** (b.1963)

(48) - *"Modern man thinks he loses something - time - when he does not do things quickly; yet he does not know what to do with the time he gains - except kill it."* **Erich Fromm** (1900-1980)

(49) - *"The Naked Ape"* (1967), 'The Human Zoo' (1969) & 'Manwatching' (1977) by **Desmond Morris** (b. 1928), zoologist, painter & popular author

(50) - *"Prayer is not an old woman's idle amusement. Properly understood and applied, it is the most potent instrument of action"* **Mohandas Gandhi** (1869-1948) - pre-eminent political and spiritual leader of India in its struggle for independence (1947)

STEP 4 - CENTERING

(51) - *"With realization of one's own potential and self-confidence in one's ability, one can build a better world"*. **The Dalai Lama** (b. 1935)

(52) - *"Primary Narcissism, in psychology is a defence mechanism, common in the formative years (6 months to 6 years old). It is intended to shield the infant and toddler from the inevitable hurt and fears involved in the individuation-separation phase of personal development. . . . The term narcissism was first used in relation to human psychology by* Sigmund Freud *after the figure of Narcissus in Greek mythology"* **Dr Sam Vaknik** (b. 1961) from 'Narcissism at a Glance'

(53) - **Sir Isaac Newton** (1643-1727) Second Law of Motion: Acceleration is proportional to the force exerted on an object, and inversely proportional to the mass. 'Philosophiae Naturalis Principia Mathematica' (1687)

"In a speed demonstration, Lee would snatch a dime off a person's open palm before they could close it, and leave a penny behind" **John Little** (b. 1955) from *'Words of the Dragon'. Interviews 1958-1973* (Bruce Lee) published in 1997.

(54) - *"Man is small, and, therefore, small is beautiful".*
E. F. Schumacher (1911-1977) from the book 'Small is Beautiful.' (1973)

"A Buddhist economist would consider this approach (belief in constant growth) excessively irrational: since consumption is merely a means to human well-being, the aim should be to obtain the maximum of well-being with the minimum of consumption.... The less toil there is, the more time and strength is left for artistic creativity. Modern economics, on the other hand, considers consumption to be the sole end and purpose of all economic activity".

(55) - *"Only in his home town, among his relatives and in his own house is a prophet without honour"* (NIV Bible) or *"A prophet is not without honour, but in his own country, and among his own kin, and in his own house"* (**King James Bible**)

(56) - *"Therefore have patience. God's promise is true. Let not those who disbelieve drive you to despair".* **The Koran** 30:60

STEP 5 - HEALING

(57) - *"In Tibet we say that many illnesses can be cured by the one medicine of love and compassion."* **The Dalai Lama** (b. 1935), 'The Medicine of Altruism', Message from his website; www.thedalailama.com

(58) - *" . . . I would say that if you have a patient or a client who has some real difficulty, psychological difficulty, look for the problem in their thinking. There is some area where they are not thinking correctly."* **M Scott-Peck** (1936-2005) American psychiatrist & bestselling author

(59) - *"Every human being is the author of his own health or disease"*. The **Buddha** (Siddhārtha Gautama) was a spiritual teacher from ancient India (6th century BC) who founded Buddhism.

(60) - *" . . We can actually correct any aggression or lack of compassion— anything anti-bodhisattva-like—as it happens; we can recognize our own neurosis and work with it, rather than trying to cover it up or throw it out. In this way one's neurotic thought pattern, or "trip," slowly dissolves. Whenever we work with our neurosis in such a direct way, it becomes compassionate action . ."* From *The Collected Works of* **Chögyam Trungpa**, *Vol. 3*, (2003) by Diana J. Mukpo

(61) - *"Man should forget his anger before he lies down to sleep"* **Mohandas Gandhi** (1869-1948)

(62) - *'Allopathic'*; literally, treatments that produce effects opposite to the symptoms and a term used by exponents of alternative medical treatments to describe traditional Western medicine

(63) - Known as Cartesian Dualism from **René Descartes** (1596-1650): 'Passions of the Soul' and 'The Description of the Human Body' (1640's)

(64) - *'Western thinking'*: Term used to describe the traditional capitalist worldview, now spread to much of the rest of the world; an admittedly crude term that represents more of a way of thinking than reference to location

(65) - *'Cartesian'*: *"of or pertaining to* **Descartes***, his mathematical methods, or his philosophy, esp. with regard to its emphasis on logical analysis and its mechanistic interpretation of physical nature."* (Dictionary.com)

(66) - 'Psychosomatic': Pertaining to the relation between mind and body," from Greek 'psykhe' = *mind* & 'somatikos' = *body*

(67) - *'Sympathetic & parasympathetic'*: *"These are fight and flight on the one hand and eating and sleeping on the other and are known as the sympathetic and parasympathetic modes respectively"*. (Step 2 Breath)

(68) - 'Immaterial' - (adjective) Definition; *"of no essential consequence; unimportant, not pertinent; irrelevant."* (Dictionary.com)

(69) - The Kiss of Judas: *"As soon as they arrived, Judas walked up to Jesus. "Rabbi!" he exclaimed, and gave him the kiss".* (Mark 14:45)

(70) - *"The vessel that gives for ever".* **Apshir Patra** (in Hindi); the notion of constant giving

(71) - *"My bounty is as boundless as the sea, my love as deep. The more I give to these the more I have, for both are infinite".* From the play 'Romeo & Juliet' (Act 2, scene 2) by **William Shakespeare** (1564-1616)

(72) - *"Work like you don't need the money. Love like you've never been hurt. Dance like nobody's watching. Sing like nobody's listening. Live like it's Heaven on Earth."* Claimed to have been written by many including Mark Twain but possibly a **Japanese proverb**.

(73) - *'Light of the sun'* - religious texts throughout history have eluded to the sun in relationship to god and love. The first well-documented example is the Egyptian Pharaoh Akhenaten (c. 1300 BC), who abandoned the many gods in favour of worshipping the 'Aten', the sun as the source of all life. **Sigmund Freud** wrote the book *'Moses & Monotheism'* (1939), suggesting that Akhenaten was the pioneer of monotheistic religion

(74) - *"A mind committed to compassion is like an overflowing reservoir - a constant source of energy, determination and kindness . . . The compassionate mind is like an elixir; it is capable of transforming bad situation into beneficial ones. Therefore, we should not limit our expressions of love and compassion to our family and friends. Nor is the compassion only the responsibility of clergy, health care and social workers. It is the necessary business of every part of the human community."* **The Dalai Lama** (b. 1935), 'The Medicine of Altruism, Messages', from his website; www.thedalailama.com

(75) - *"All that we are is the result of what we have thought. If a man speaks or acts with an evil thought, pain follows him. If a man speaks or acts with a pure thought, happiness follows him, like a shadow that never leaves him".* **The Buddha** (c. 563-483 BC)

STEP 6 - RESPECTING

(76) - *"I am a Muslim and a Hindu and a Christian and a Jew and so are all of you"*. From the film 'Gandhi' (Screenplay by **John Briley**) about the Indian political and spiritual leader (1869 - 1948)

(77) - *"But I say unto you, Love your enemies, bless them that curse you, do good to them that hate you, and pray for them which despitefully use you, and persecute you"*. The New Testament, **St James Bible**; Matthew 5:44

(78) - *"To know a man you must know his history"*
Mark Twain (1835-1910)

(79) - *"I have no desire to make windows into men's souls"* **Queen Elizabeth I of England** (1533-1603)

(80) - *"Today, millions of people in America & Europe try to find contact with tradition and with teachers that can show them the way. But in large part the doctrines and teachers are either fraudulent or vitiated by the spirit of public relations ballyhoo, or mixed up with the financial or prestige interests of the respective gurus."* **Erich Fromm** (1900-1980), from *'To Have or To Be?'* (1976)

(81) - *"a little knowledge is a dangerous thing"*: probably **Alexander Pope** (1688 - 1744)

(82) - *"The British biologist and atheist Richard Dawkins believes that altruism in modern humans is essentially an evolutionary oops, albeit a beneficial one. It paid off in prehistory, when people lived in clans and protecting others meant the survival of their own gene pools; now that we've expanded into large cities, our instinct to help others still kicks in, even though those we aid may have no relation to us"*: **Rich Barlow** (for the Richard Dawkins Foundation)

(83) - *"To the Jews who had believed him, Jesus said, "If you hold to my teaching, you are really my disciples. Then you will know the truth, and the truth will set you free. "* **Jesus Christ**, quoted by St John the Evangelist 8:31

(84) - *"So, in the light of this vision, respect would mean seeing beyond the body - whether plant, animal, insect, human (black/white, young/old etc.) - to the real person who is the soul. That way you have*

tremendous respect for the equality and rights of every tiny creature as an eternal part or spark of the whole spirit (God). When you 'see' the soul you don't have to get caught up in judging anyone, or feeling better or worse than anyone." **Kaliyphani** (b. 1953) is one of the original disciples of A. C. Bhaktivedanta Swami Prabhupada (the founder of the International Society for Krishna Consciousness).

(85) - *" . . . In order to arrive at what you do not know, You must go by a way which is the way of ignorance."* **T. S. Elliot,** from the poem 'East Coker' *"You say I am repeating Something I have said before. I shall say it again. Shall I say it again? In order to arrive there, To arrive where you are, to get from where you are not, You must go by a way wherein there is no ecstasy. In order to arrive at what you do not know, You must go by a way which is the way of ignorance. In order to possess what you do not possess, You must go by the way of dispossession. In order to arrive at what you are not, You must go through the way in which you are not. And what you do not know is the only thing you know, And what you own is what you do not own And where you are is where you are not."*

STEP 7 - FORGIVING

(86) - *"An eye for an eye only ends up making the whole world blind."* **Mohandas Gandhi** (1869-1948)

(87) - *"Come now, let us reason together,"* says the Lord. *"Though your sins are like scarlet, they shall be as white as snow; though they are red as crimson, they shall be like wool."* (Isaiah : 1:18 NIV). *"For I desire mercy, not sacrifice, and acknowledgment of God rather than burnt offerings."* (Hosea - 6:6 / NIV) Reference kindly provided by Rev. Dr Zeev Amit (United Synagogues UK)

(88) - *" . . . the Most Gracious, the Most Merciful, and the Most Beneficent"* and is more merciful to His creatures than a mother to her child". **The Prophet Muhammad** (570-632)

(89) - **Chowdhury Mueen-Uddin**, A founder of the Muslim Council of Britain (2009-2010) & former secretary general of the Council of Mosques UK & Eire (1984-1988); *"Say: O My servants who have*

transgressed against their own souls, despair not of the mercy of Allah. Indeed, Allah forgives all sins. Truly, He is Most Forgiving, Most Merciful." Verse of the Holy Quran (Surah az-Zumar 39:53)

"*O son of Adam, as long as you call upon Me and put your hope in Me, I have forgiven you for what you have done and I do not mind. O son of Adam, if your sins were to reach the clouds of the sky and then you would seek My forgiveness, I would forgive you. O son of Adam, if you were to come to Me with sins that are close to filling the earth and then you would meet Me without ascribing any partners with Me, I would certainly bring to you forgiveness close to filling it.*"

Hadithi Qudsi, Prophet Muhammad's direct quote from Allah (but not part of the text of the Quran).

(90) - "*. . . We are first to acknowledge our "sins" against others, and then make reparations. In turn, we ask for forgiveness and it is expected that just as each of us hopes that others will forgive us, we are expected to forgive others for their sins against us. Thereafter, we can turn to our failures in our relationship with God. We are assured that if we are sincere in our repentance, then God will forgive us*". **Rabbi Lerner** (b. 1943)

"*I know that there is no one so righteous that they have not wronged another, financially or physically, through deed or speech. This pains my heart within me, because wrongs between humans and their fellow are not atoned by Yom Kippur, until the wronged one is appeased. Because of this, my heart breaks within me, and my bones tremble; for even the day of death does not atone for such sins. Therefore I prostrate and beg before You, to have mercy on me, and grant me grace, compassion, and mercy in Your eyes and in the eyes of all people. For behold, I forgive with a final and resolved forgiveness anyone who has wronged me, whether in person or property, even if they slandered me, or spread falsehoods against me. So I release anyone who has injured me either in person or in property, or has committed any manner of sin that one may commit against another [except for legally enforceable business obligations, and except for someone who has deliberately harmed me with the thought 'I can harm him because he will forgive me']. Except for* these two, I fully and finally forgive everyone; may no one be punished because of me. And just as I forgive everyone, so may You grant me grace in the eyes of others, that they too forgive me absolutely." Closing of the **Tefila Zaka** meditation, recited before Yom Kippur

(91) - "It is forbidden to be obdurate and not allow yourself to be appeased. On the contrary, one should be easily pacified and find it difficult to become angry. When asked by an offender for forgiveness, one should forgive with a sincere mind and a willing spirit. . . forgiveness is natural to the seed of Israel. " **Mishneh Tora** (Teshuvah 2:10)

(92) - The Parable of the Prodigal Son (Luke 15:11-32)

(93) - The Parable of the unforgiving servant (Matthew 18:21-32)

(94) - "Blessed are the merciful, for they will be shown mercy. " (Matthew 5:7)

(95) - "If someone strikes you on one cheek, turn to him the other also. " (Luke 6:27-29, NIV)

(96) - "Be merciful, just as your Father is merciful. " (Luke 6:36, NIV)

(97) - "Do not judge, and you will not be judged. Do not condemn, and you will not be condemned. Forgive, and you will be forgiven. " (Luke 6:37, NIV)

(98) - "If men who are fighting hit a pregnant woman and she gives birth prematurely, but there is no serious injury, the offender must be fined whatever the woman's husband demands and the court allows. But if there is serious injury, you are to take life for life, eye for eye, tooth for tooth, hand for hand, foot for foot." (Exodus 21:22)

(99) - 'The Theory of Altruism'. Notion that altruism is merely genes assisting their own type to progress, as outlined in the book 'The Selfish Gene' (1976) by **Prof. Richard Dawkins** (b, 1941)

(100) - **Rabbi Shraga Simmons** (b. 1961) is the senior editor of Aish.com and the director of JewishPathways.com. He is also regarded as an expert on media bias relating to the Middle East conflict, and was the founding editor of HonestReporting.com. Written in aish.com. (Launched in February 2000)

(101) - "The sacrifices of God are a broken spirit, a broken and a contrite heart, these O God, You will not despise." (Psalm. 51:17, NIV).

These words are part of a confessional prayer of king David, after he had committed a grievous sin.

(102) - *"Judge not, that ye be not judged. For with what judgment ye judge, ye shall be judged: and with what measure ye mete, it shall be measured to you again. And why beholdest thou the mote that is in thy brother's eye, but considerest not the beam that is in thine own eye? Or how wilt thou say to thy brother, Let me pull out the mote out of thine eye; and, behold, a beam is in thine own eye? Thou hypocrite, first cast out the beam out of thine own eye; and then shalt thou see clearly to cast out the mote out of thy brother's eye."* **Matthew 7:1-5** (King James Version)

(103) - *"The Roman Church will tell you, if you do this you'll go there, if you do that you'll go someplace else. It feels as if you're arriving at Heathrow Airport. But we don't know the judgment of God - no-one knows".* **Sir John Tavener** (b.1944). British composer

(104) - *"If you judge people, you have no time to love them".* **Mother Teresa of Calcutta** (1910 - 1997) - Albanian born Indian missionary and founder of the Order of the Missionaries of Charity. Winner of Nobel Prize for Peace (1979)

(105)- *"What goes around, comes around"* Old un-attributed saying. Possibly part of: *"Dance like nobody's watching; love like you've never been hurt. Sing like nobody's listening; live like it's heaven on earth."* **Mark Twain**? (1835-1910)

(106) - *"The weak can never forgive. Forgiveness is the attribute of the strong."* **Mohandas Gandhi** (1869-1948)

(107) - *"naham vipro na ca nara-patir napi vaisyo na sudro naham varni na ca grha-patir no vanastho yatir va kintu prodyan nikhila-paramananda-purnamrtabdher gopi-bhartuh pada-kamalayor dasa-dasanudasah"* (Padyavali,) *"trinad api Sunicena, taror api Sahisnuna, amanina manadena, kirtaniya sada hari"* Translation: *"To be more humble then a blade of grass, to be more tolerant than a tree, Always give respect to others and expect none in return, In that state of mind one can chant the Holy Names constantly".*

(108) - *"I am not a brahmana (priest or Vedic scholar), ksatriya (warrior or administrator), vaisya (agriculturalist or businessman), or sudra (worker), nor a brahmacari (celibate student), grhastha*

(householder), vanaprastha (renounced householder) or sannyasi (full renunciate). Being transcendental to this gross and subtle body, I am the servant of the servant of the servant of the lotus feet of the master of the gopis, Sri Krsna, who is the ultimate shelter of everyone, full of transcendental bliss and an ocean of unlimited nectar"

(109) - *"Forgiveness then becomes effortless; "Forgive them Lord, they know not what they do."* (Reference from New Testament - Luke 23:34) . . *. that is not condescending but spoken from a platform of real knowledge."* **Kaliyaphani**

(110) - *"Forgiveness liberates the soul. It removes fear. That is why it is such a powerful weapon".* From the film 'Invictus'. Story based on the book *'Playing the Enemy'* by **John Carlin** (b.1956)

STEP 8 - RESOLVING

(111) - *"Hatred does not cease by hatred, but only by love; this is the eternal rule"* **The Buddha** (c. 563-483 BC)

(112) - *"Real freedom means freedom from fear".* **Aung San Suu Kyi** (b. 1945) quoted by Fergal Keane (b. 1961), the Irish writer & broadcaster, from an interview following her release from house arrest in 1995

(113) - *"Only the dictatorship of the proletariat and the poor peasants is capable of smashing the resistance of the capitalists . . Power to the Soviets - this is the only way to make further progress gradual, peaceful and smooth . . "* **Vladimir Ilyich Lenin** (1917) Note: The violent word 'smashing', reminds the author of words such as 'crush', used on government billboards in Burma today, with reference to 'enemies' of the state

(114) - *"People were bringing little children to Jesus for him to place his hands on them, but the disciples rebuked them. 14 When Jesus saw this, he was indignant. He said to them, "Let the little children come to me, and do not hinder them, for the kingdom of God belongs to such as these. 15 Truly I tell you, anyone who will not receive the kingdom of God like a little child will never enter it." 16 And he took*

the children in his arms, placed his hands on them and blessed them." **Jesus Christ** (Mark 10:13-16, NIV)

(115) - Evidence of the 'culture of submissiveness' in the media can be found in *reality-shows* forcing participants to submit, such as standing vulnerably while receiving the ruling of their 'superiors'. Another example might be a drama that portrays gratuitous social or sexual humiliation. Men have not escaped being the politically correct targets of much denigration in this respect.

(116) - "*The mystery of his life still eludes us, the shadows move but the dark never quite dispersed*" **Howard Carter** (1874-1939), who, after 15 years of searching with Lord Carnarvon, discovered the tomb of Tutankhamun in the Valley of the Kings Nov. 1922.

(117) - "*Never let your enmity for anyone lead you into the sin of deviating from justice. Always be just: that is closest to being God-fearing.*" **Qur'an, al-Ma'idah 5:8.**

(118) - "*If might is right, then love has no place in the world. It may be so, it may be so. But I don't have the strength to live in a world like that*". Father Gabriel to Rodrigo, from the film *'The Mission'*. (1986) Screenplay by **Robert Bold** (1924-1995)

STEP 9 - LEADING

(119) - "*I suppose leadership at one time meant muscles; but today it means getting along with people.*" **Mohandas Gandhi** (1869-1948)

(120) - "*Let both sides explore what problems unite us instead of belabouring those problems which divide us.*" **John F. Kennedy** from speech at the Berlin Wall (1962)

(121) - "*You fail if you don't try. If you try and you fail, yes, you'll have a few articles saying you've failed at something. But if you look at the history of American entrepreneurs, one thing I do know about them: An awful lot of them have tried and failed in the past and gone on to great things.*" **Richard Branson** (b. 1950). British entrepreneur who heads the Virgin group of over 400 companies.

(122) - *"Success is 10 percent inspiration and 90 percent perspiration."* **Thomas Edison** (1847-1931) America's most famous inventor, with over 1,000 patents to his name

(123) - The Rembrandt Research Project (started 1968) by the Netherlands Organization for the Advancement of Scientific Research, aimed to create a full catalogue of his works. But in the scientific process, it reassigned many works previously considered by his hand, to his students and followers, with dramatic consequences for collections around the world

(124) - *"Do not wait for leaders; do it alone, person to person."* **Mother Teresa** (1910-1997)

(125) - *"Out of the night that covers me, Black as the pit from pole to pole, I thank whatever gods may be, For my unconquerable soul. In the fell clutch of circumstance, I have not winced nor cried aloud. Under the bludgeonings of chance, My head is bloody, but unbowed. Beyond this place of wrath and tears, Looms but the Horror of the shade, And yet the menace of the years, Finds and shall find me unafraid. It matters not how strait the gate, How charged with punishments the scroll, I am the master of my fate: I am the captain of my soul."* Poem 'Invictus' by **William E Henley** (1849-1903). Henley contracted tuberculosis of the bone, requiring the amputation of one leg at the knee when he was 12. The poem was quoted in the film of the same name about Nelson Mandela, directed by Clint Eastwood (2009)

(126) - *"Strength does not come from physical capacity. It comes from an indomitable will"* **Mohandas Gandhi** was working in South Africa from 1893 to 1914, before returning to India

(127) - *'The Road Less Travelled'* (1978). The title of a book by M Scott-Peck, based on the poem by **Robert Frost** (1874-1963). *'The Road Not Taken'* (1916) *" . . I shall be telling this with a sigh Somewhere ages and ages hence: Two roads diverged in a wood, and I-- I took the one less travelled by, And that has made all the difference."* (Final Verse)

(128) - *"I ask so much confidence only as may give firmness and effect to the legal administration of your affairs. I shall often go wrong through*

defect of judgment . . I ask your indulgence of my own errors, which will never be intentional . . " **Thomas Jefferson** (1743-1826), from his inaugural address (1801)

(129) - *"As we are liberated from our own fear, our presence automatically liberates others."* **Nelson Mandela** (b.1918)

(130) - Jesus Christ, Mohandas Gandhi, Martin Luther King (& Princess Diana, some allege, possibly for campaigning against land mines)

(131) - *"Security, sense of identity and confidence based on faith in what one is, on one's need for relatedness, interest, love, solidarity with the world around us, instead on one's desire to have, to possess, to control the world, and thus become the slave of one's possessions."* **Erich Fromm** (1900-1980) from the book 'To Have or To Be?' *(1976)*

(132) - *"I have learned that a strong man has no need of power & a weak man is destroyed by it."* The words of Tzar Nicholas II from the book *'Nicholas & Alexandra'* by **Robert K Massie** (made into a film in 1971, directed by Franklin J Schaffner)

STEP 10 - PEACE

(133) - " Peace starts with a smile". **Mother Teresa** (1910-1997). Albanian Catholic & founder of The Missionaries of Charity in Calcutta

(134) - *"Every time you smile at someone, it is an action of love, a gift to that person, a beautiful thing"* **Mother Teresa** (1910-1997)

(135) - *"Small is Beautiful"* by **E F Schumacher** (1911-1977) Economist. Considered by the Times Literary Supplement as one of the most influential books since WWII

(136) - 'integral transformation practice', from the book 'A Theory of Everything' (2000) by **Ken Wilber** (b. 1949)

(137) - Known as 'Cartesian Dualism' from **René Descartes** (1596-1650), 'Passions of the Soul' and 'The Description of the Human Body' (1640's)

(138) - Example: 'The Tao of Physics' (1975), by the physicist **Fritjof Capra** (b. 1939). Exploring the connections between modern physics and Eastern Mysticism

(139) - 'War and Peace' (1869). Novel by **Leo Tolstoy** (1828-1910), about the events leading up to the Napoleonic invasion of Russia. Also, Gandhi quoted in 1942 *"This war is showing the futility of violence"*

(140) - *"The just war"* laid out by **St Augustine** in 'On the City of God' (5th century AD) and taken up by Medieval thinkers such as Thomas Aquinas

(141) - **St. Thomas Aquinas** (1225-1274), wrote 'The Summa Theologica' (1265-1274). Aquinus was a 13th century theologian and philosopher with great influence on the Christian Church

(142) - *"One of the aspects of traditional just war theory is that you need to know what would count as a good end and how you would know when you have that and what to do then . . .I don't think we had that in place sadly. I don't think we knew what we would do next or what would count as our ending. And that is the tragedy."* Spoken by **Dr Rowan Williams** (Archbishop of Canterbury) to 600 church leaders on the eve of Remembrance Sunday 11th November 2007

(143) - *"Iraq war logs reveal 15,000 previously unlisted civilian deaths. Leaked Pentagon files contain records of more than 100,000 fatalities including 66,000 civilians."* **David Leigh,** writing in The Guardian (22nd October 2010)

(144) - *"Britain's Trillion Pound Horror Story"*. A Channel 4 documentary (11th Nov. 2010) by **Martin Durkin**

(145) - **Luke Hughes** (b. 1957) is a leading furniture designer and an authority on timber & sustainable forestry. Quotes taken from his company blog; www.lukehughes.co.uk/index.php/blog

(146) - *"The war to end all war"*. The British author & commentator **H G Wells** (1866-1946) used the expression in 1914 to describe the 1st World War and the desperate hope of the time

(147) - *"Land-mines are uniquely savage in the history of modern conventional warfare not only because of their appalling individual impact, but also their long-term social and economic destruction (Ms. Machel) . . . Children in at least 68 countries are today*

threatened by what may be the most toxic pollution facing mankind — the contamination by mines of the land they live on. Over 110 million land-mines of various types — plus millions more unexploded bombs, shells and grenades — remain hidden around the world, waiting to be triggered by the innocent and unsuspecting, the report says. Once laid, a mine may remain active for up to 50 years. Unless vigorous action is taken, mines placed today will still be killing and maiming people well into the middle of the next century. In just one district of Viet Nam 300 children have died, 42 have lost one or more limbs, and 16 have been blinded as a result of land-mines laid during the Viet Nam war. As one Khmer Rouge general put it, a land-mine is the most excellent of soldiers, for it is "ever courageous, never sleeps, never misses." **UNICEF** - *(Impact of Armed Conflict on Children).*

(148) - *"Children in at least 68 countries are today threatened by what may be the most toxic pollution facing mankind — the contamination by mines of the land they live on. Over 110 million land-mines of various types — plus millions more unexploded bombs, shells and grenades — remain hidden around the world, waiting to be triggered by the innocent and unsuspecting, the report says. So common are mines in Cambodia that they are now used for fishing, to protect private property and even to settle private disputes."* **UNICEF (www.unicef.org/graca/mines.htm)**

(149) - *"From Stettin in the Baltic to Trieste in the Adriatic an iron curtain has descended across the continent."* **Winston S Churchill** (1875-1965), spoken in 1945

(150) - *'I am a soldier, convinced that I am acting on behalf of soldiers. I believe that this war, upon which I entered as a war of defence and liberation, has now become a war of aggression and conquest. I have seen and endured the sufferings of the troops, and I can no longer be a party to prolong those sufferings for ends which I believe to be evil and unjust. I am not protesting against the conduct of the war, but against the political errors and insincerities for which the fighting men are being sacrificed. On behalf of those who are suffering now I make this protest against the deception*

which is being practised on them.   Also I believe that I may help to destroy the callous complacence with which the majority of those at home regard the continuance of agonies which they do not share, and which they have not sufficient imagination to realise.'
Siegfried Sassoon's (1886-1967). From his 1917 'Statement'

(151) - *"What branches grow out of this stony rubbish?"* **T.S. Elliot** (1888-1965), from the poem 'The Waste Land', written in the aftermath of the 1st World War (1922) *"April is the cruellest month, breeding lilacs out of the dead land, mixing memory and desire, stirring dull roots with spring rain."*

(152) - *"When you're young, it sounds exciting, war; shooting people. It's not exciting at all, it's a dirty business"*. **Jack Taylor** (1st Para Brigade - Arnhem 1944), speaking on Remembrance Sunday (2010)

(153) - *"War is like a fire in the human community, one whose fuel is living beings."* *"Since armies are legal, we feel that war is acceptable; in general, nobody feels that war is criminal or that accepting it is a criminal attitude. In fact, we have been brainwashed. War is neither glamorous nor attractive. It is monstrous. Its very nature is one of tragedy and suffering."* *"After the officer in charge have given beautiful explanations about the importance of the army, its discipline and the need to conquer the enemy, the rights of the great mass of soldiers are most entirely taken away. They are then compelled to forfeit their individual will, and, in the end, to sacrifice their lives. Moreover, once an army has become a powerful force, there is every risk that it will destroy the happiness of its own country."* **The Dalai Lama** (b. 1935), from 'The Reality of War', Messages from his website; www.thedalailama.com

(154) - **Jesus Christ** on Peace: *"But I say to you that hear, Love your enemies, do good to those who hate you, bless those who curse you, pray for those who abuse you.   If you love those who love you, what credit is that to you?   For even sinners love those who love them. And if you do good to those who do good to you, what credit is that to you?   For even sinners do the same."* Luke 6:27-32
"Then Peter came up and said to him, "Lord, how often shall my brother sin against me, and I forgive him? As many as seven times?"

Jesus said to him, "I do not say to you seven times, but seventy times seven..." Matt 18:21-22

"Blessed are the meek, for they shall inherit the earth... Blessed are the merciful, for they shall obtain mercy... Blessed are the peacemakers, for they shall be called sons of God". Matt 5:5-9

"Then Jesus said to him, "Put your sword back into its place; for those who live by the sword, die by the sword". Matt 26:52

"You have heard that it was said, 'An eye for an eye and a tooth for a tooth.' But I tell you, do not resist an evil person. If someone strikes you on the right cheek, turn to him the other also. And if someone wants to sue you and take your tunic, let him have your cloak as well. If someone forces you to go one mile, go with him two miles. Give to the one who asks you, and do not turn away from the one who wants to borrow from you." **Jesus Christ** quoted in the Gospel of St Matthew 5:38-42 (NIV). Same doctrine and similar words in St Marks' Gospel (6:27-31 NIV)

(155) - The dangers of ideological compromise are illustrated by the example of the history of Green Peace. Rather than risk their principles, Greenpeace risked bankruptcy and the resulting sympathy provided the funding to buy the first ship, Rainbow Warrior. See; *'Greenpeace, the Inside Story'* (2004) by **Rex Weyler** (b. 1947 - director of the original Greenpeace Foundation, the editor of the organisation's first newsletter, and a cofounder of Greenpeace)

(156) - *"The greatest mistake ever made by Rome".* From the book 'The Robe' by **Lloyd C Douglas** (1877-1951)

(157) - *"Non-violence is the greatest force at the disposal of mankind. It is mightier than the mightiest weapon of destruction devised by the ingenuity of man."* **Mohandas Gandhi** (1869-1948)

(158) - During the War of the Spanish Succession (1701-1714), the much admired general, Prince Eugene's dispatches included the words; *"our men did things the Turkish way, cutting off their testicles and giving no quarter"* from; *'Blenheim, Battle for Europe'* by **Charles Spencer** (b. 1964, brother of Princess Diana)

(159) - *"Si vis pacem, para bellum"* from **Flavius Vegetius Renatus** (c. 375 AD): *"If you want peace, prepare for war"*

(160) - The US alone spent $663 billion on 'defence' in 2009. Quoted in the Telegraph (9/11/10) Sources: SIPRI and IISS

(161) - *"The gun is always there for use . . . we are convinced that the non-violent approach is best"* **Aung San Suu Kyi** (b. 1945). Aung San Suu Kyi is the Burmese pro-democracy opposition leader, who has spend over 14 years in prison or house arrest.

(162) - *"Instead, why not leave India to her own resources and thereby gain a moral victory before the world and be saved the ignominy of a very probably disaster."* **Mohandas Gandhi** (1869-1948), quoted by T. A. Raman in his book 'What does Gandhi Want' (1942)

(163) - *"Estimates for the total casualties of the war vary, because many deaths went unrecorded. Most suggest that some 60 million people died in the war, including about 20 million soldiers and 40 million civilians. Many civilians died because of decease, starvation, massacre, bombing and deliberate genocide. The Soviet Union lost around 27 million people during the war, almost half of all World War II deaths. One of every four Soviet citizens was killed or wounded in that war".* (Source: 'The World's Wasted Wealth 2, Save our Wealth, Save our Environment' by **J. W. Smith**, forward by Robert Swann (President of the Schumacher Society)

(164) - *"Si vis pacem para pacem"* = *"If you want peace, prepare for peace."* From The National Arbitration and Peace Congress of 1907, presided over by **Andrew Carnegie** (1835-1919); *"These vast armaments on land and water are being defended as a means, not to wage war, but to prevent war.... there is a safer way ... it requires only the consent and the good-will of the governments. Today they say .... If you want peace, prepare for war. This Congress says in behalf of the people: Si vis pacem, para pactum, if you want peace, agree to keep the peace"*

(165) - *" . . . For even as we celebrate tonight, we know the challenges that tomorrow will bring are the greatest of our lifetime - two wars, a planet in peril, the worst financial crisis in a century . . tonight we proved once more that the true strength of our nation comes not from the might of our arms or the scale of our wealth, but from the enduring power of our ideas; democracy, liberty, opportunity, and*

unyielding hope." **Barack Obama** (b. 1961). Speech after winning US presidential election, 4th November 2008

(166) - **Mikhail Sergeyevich Gorbachev** (b. 1931). General Secretary of the Communist Party of the Soviet Union (1985-1991) and last head of state of the USSR (1988-1991). Awarded the Nobel Peace Price in 1990

(167) - *"For peace has its victories more glorious than those of war. The non-violent method would have meant no abject surrender. It would have confounded all modern tactics of war, indeed rendered them of no use."* **Mohandas Gandhi (1869-1948),** quoted in the book 'What does Gandhi Want' (1942).

(168) - *". . . my son, like thousands of other Muslim boys, spends hours blasting away at his own people. . "* (with American video games such as; *"Muslim massacre"; "War in the Gulf"; "Conflict: Total Terror"*). **Aijaz Afaqui** reporting in News International (Karachi - Oct 2010).

(169) - *"If you want to make peace with your enemy, you have to work with your enemy. Then he becomes your partner".* **Nelson Mandela** (b. 1918)

(170) - *". . . no one can build his happiness at the expense of the misery of others. . the call for permanent and just peace, based on respect for the UN resolutions, has now become the call of the whole world"* **Anwar Al-Sadat** (1918-1981). Speech to the Israeli Knesset, 20th November 1977 (assassinated)

(171) - *"Liberty and democracy become unholy when their hands are dyed red with innocent blood."* **Mohandas Gandhi** (1869-1948), quoted by T A Raman in his book 'What does Gandhi Want'.

(172) - *"It is not power that corrupts but fear. Fear of losing power corrupts those who wield it and fear of the scourge of power corrupts those who are subject to it."* **Aung San Suu Kyi** (b. 1945) from her speech 'Freedom From Fear' (1990)

(173) - *"No one who believes in non-violence, as a creed, need, therefore, sit still . . I stress only one condition, namely, let our pledge of truth and non-violence as the only means for the attainment of (home*

rule) be faithfully kept." **Mohandas Gandhi** (1869-1948). From speech on the eve of his 'Salt Marches' (1930)

(174) - *"Without a revolution of the spirit, the forces which produced the iniquities of the old order would continue to be operative, posing a constant threat to the process of reform and regeneration. It is not enough merely to call for freedom, democracy and human rights. There has to be a united determination to persevere in the struggle, to make sacrifices in the name of enduring truths, to resist the corrupting influences of desire, ill will, ignorance and fear".* **Aung San Suu Kyi** (b. 1945). Spoken in 2010

(175) - 'An integral vision'. From the book by **Ken Wilber** (b. 1949); 'A Theory of Everything. An integral Vision for Business, Politics, Science and Spirituality' (first published by Gateway in 2001)

(176) - *"The whole course of human development can be viewed as a continuing decline in egocentrism".* The Harvard developmental psychologist **Howard Gardner**, quoted by Ken Wilber in "The Theory of Everything" (2001); *"Thus development, for the most part, involves decreasing narcisism and increasing consciousness, or the ability to make other people, places and things into account and thus increasingly extend care to each . . move from ethnocentric to worldcentric, from dominator social hierarchies towards meritocracies, from duty to dignity"*

(177) - 'Ethics for the New Millennium' (1999) by the **Dalai Lama** (b. 1935) Buddhist leader of the Tibetans.

(178) - ". . . *a real man will never let his fear of death overpower his honour, his sense of duty to his country and his innate manhood. Battle is the most magnificent competition in which a human being can indulge."* **General George S Patten** (1885-1945). Speech to 3rd Army before D-Day 5th June 1944

(179) - *"In the process of gaining our rightful place we must not be guilty of wrongful deeds. Let us not seek to satisfy our thirst for freedom by drinking from the cup of bitterness and hatred. We must ever conduct our struggle on the high plane of dignity and discipline. We must not allow our creative protest to degenerate into physical violence. Again and again we must rise to the majestic heights of*

meeting physical force with soul force" **Martin Luther King, Jr.**
(1929-1968). Civil rights speech from the Lincoln Memorial (1963)

(180) - *"Thus to provide the people with the protective coolness of peace and security, rulers must observe the teachings of the Buddha. Central to these teachings are the concepts of truth, righteousness and loving kindness. It is government based on these very qualities that the people of Burma are seeking."* **Aung San Suu Kyi** (b. 1945)

(181) - *"What will the legacy of this vanishing century be? . . Surely it will be judged, and judged severely in both moral and metaphysical terms . .So much violence, so much indifference".* Millennium speech (12th April 1999) **Elie Wiesel** (b.1928). Survivor of Auschwitz, Nobel Peace Prize winner (1986) and founder of the Elie Wiesel Foundation for Humanity

(182) - *" . . . I think it is true to say that atomic weapons are a peril which affect everyone in the world, and in that sense a completely common problem . . I think that in order to handle this common problem there must be a complete sense of community responsibility . . the point I want to make, the one point I want to hammer home, is what an enormous change of spirit is involved. . . We cannot forget our dependence on our fellow men"* **J Robert Oppenheimer** (1904-1967). Chairman of the board of the scientific advisers of the Atomic Energy Commission (1947-1952) From a speech made in 1945, before losing security clearance (1953)

(183) - *"A small body of determined spirits fired by an unquenchable faith in their mission can alter the course of history"*
Mohandas Gandhi (1869-1948).

CONCLUSION

(184) - *". . . So non-violence to her is about love"* **Alan Clement.** Canadian writer & former Buddhist monk who wrote 'The Voice of Hope' from conversations with Aung San Suu Kyi

(185) - Vast amounts of international data is available but the California Coalition Against Sexual Assault (**CALCASA**) undertook detailed

research at Stanford University in the 1990s. Their findings included: *"1 in 4 women had been victims of rape or attempted rape. 84% of those raped knew their attacker, and 57% of the rapes happened on dates. Only 27% of the women whose sexual assault met the legal definition of rape thought of themselves as rape victims. 42% of the rape victims told no one about the assault, and only 5% reported it to the police About 75% of the men and at least 55% of the women involved in acquaintance rapes had been drinking or taking drugs just before the attack. According to the National Institute of Justice, rape is the costliest crime in the U.S., exacting $86,500 in tangible and intangible costs per victim. Results of a 1997 study of sexual coercion within gay and lesbian relationships indicated that 52% of the total sample reported having experienced at least one incident of sexual coercion. 55% of the gay men and 50% of the lesbians in this study reported unwanted penetration. 33% of the gay men and 32% of the lesbians in this study reported unwanted fondling. In 1992, the National Victim Centre reported that 9 out of 10 rapes go unreported"*

(186) - *". . assumption was, that what was good for the "system", for big corporations, was good for man, as man was innately egotistic, selfish & greedy, therefore man was being "natural".* **Erich Fromm** (1900-1980), from his book 'To Have or to Be?' (1976)

(187) - *"We hesitate not at all at leaving our own descendants this plundered earth as their heritage"* **Erich Fromm** (1900-1980), from his book; 'To Have or to Be?' (1976)

(188) - The author remembers a particular encounter with such an indigenous people in the Peruvian jungle near Maldonado in the 1980s and was struck by their remarkable gentleness. However, it is perhaps appropriate to qualify this observation with the opinion of the renowned war correspondent & writer **Kate Adie** (b. 1945), who told the author that in her experience, simple peoples can have limited understanding between gentleness & violence & can flip from one state to the other with little provocation

(189) - *"It is ironic that the more serious problems emanate from the more industrially advanced societies. Science and technology have worked*

wonders in many fields, but the basic human problems remain. There is unprecedented literacy, yet this universal education does not seem to have fostered goodness, but only mental restlessness and discontent instead." **The Dalai Lama** (b. 1935), from 'A Human Approach to peace', Messages from his website: www.thedalailama.com

(190) - *"(See is in) the grips of a global catastrophe, a global nightmare . . The ordinary people out there - there is something missing in their lives, they can't articulate exactly what it is, but they are searching."* *"Having in our minds desanctified ourselves, we have also desanctified the natural world in our minds. This self-image and world view have their origin in our loss of memory, in our forgetfulness of who we are, and in our fall to a level of ignorance and stupidity that threatens the survival of our race."* **Sir John Tavener** (b. 1944), British composer

(191) - *"didn't believe the so-called 'War on Terror' was winnable in a military sense."* Director General of MI5 (2002-2010), **Baroness Manningham-Buller** (b. 1948), Quoted on BBC's 'The Secret War on Terror' (21/3/11)

(192) - *"The UK-based defence industry employs over 300,000 people and generated over £35 billion in turnover and £7.2 billion in exports in 2009."* Quoted from the Telegraph (11/3/11)

(193) - It is a brave man that questions the heroic profile of Sir Winston Churchill in the West & particularly Britain and it is not the author's intention to malign this remarkable and much loved figure. His family likewise, has functioned in difficult circumstances and while not all the Marlborough's have been equally distinguished, the present (11th) Duke is regarded by those close to him as an exception, working tirelessly to preserve the heavy burden of his inheritance & responsibilities

(194) - *"I feel so lonely without a war"*. **Winston Churchill** (1874-1965), recalled by Lord Moran (1945) & quoted by Marian Fowler in her book 'Blenheim: Biography of a Palace' (1989). Lord Moran was the title of Charles Wilson, Churchill's personal physician during the war

(195) - **Ashoka** (304-232BC) Emperor of most of the Indian Subcontinent, following the 'victory' of the Kalinga War & before his conversion to Buddhism & adoption of non-violence; *"What have I done? If this is a victory, what's a defeat then? Is this a victory or a defeat? Is this justice or injustice? Is it gallantry or a rout? Is it valour to kill innocent children and women? Do I do it to widen the empire and for prosperity or to destroy the other's kingdom and splendour? One has lost her husband, someone else a father, someone a child, someone an unborn infant.... What's this debris of the corpses? Are these marks of victory or defeat? Are these vultures, crows, eagles the messengers of death or evil?"*

(196) - *". . . If any resistance is to be offered by the many to the few, it must be offered in a field in which technological superiority does not count . . . that (we) will be able to extort liberty from a ruling minority equipped by science with the very latest in self-propelled flame-throwers and atomic missiles seems in the highest degree unlikely. It is in satyagraha, or non-violent direct action, that the only hope of future revolutions resides."* And went on to say; *"The pen and the word are at least as mighty as the sword; for the sword is wielded in obedience to the spoken or written word."*
Aldous Huxley (1894-1963), author of 'Brave New World'

(197) - 'From Dictatorship to Democracy' (1993) by **Dr Gene Sharp** (b. 1928)

(198) - *"One of the main points which we used was Sharp's idea of identifying a regime's pillars of support,"* he said. *"If we could build a relationship with the army, Mubarak's biggest pillar of support, to get them on our side, then we knew he would quickly be finished."*
Ruaridh Arrow - director of the film *'Gene Sharp - How to Start a Revolution'* quoting an activist in the 2011 Egyptian uprising (BBC Online 21/2/11)

(199) - *"You saying that your culture and morals are in danger of being destroyed leads one to think that the reform movement in your country was only skin-deep . . Blaming the wolf (Japan), would not help the sheep much. The sheep must learn not to fall into the clutches of the wolf"*. **Mohandas Gandhi** (1869-1948)

(200) - *"I suggest that at the end of the war, whichever way it ends, there will be no democracy left to represent democracy . . It is a warning that if nobody reads the writing on the wall, man will be reduced to the state of the beast, whom he is shaming by his manners."*
Mohandas Gandhi (1869-1948)

(201) - "(Change in Burma), *will have to come from inside"* **Kate Adie** (b. 1945), World-renowned war correspondent & commentator, in conversation with the author (4/7/11).

(202) - Gallop asked for a 'yes or no' answer to; "Are you in favour of the war in Iraq": In Britain: Under no circumstances = 41%, Only if sanctioned by the UN = 39%, Unilaterally by the US & allies = 10%. In France 60% answered 'under no circumstances'. Source: Gallop International, 'Iraq Survey' January 2003

(203) - In March 2011 News Corporation bid for the remaining 61% of BSkyB, giving it a huge stake in the British media. In a move that surprised many, the Culture Minister of the British coalition government (Jeremy Hunt) allowed this important development without considering it necessary for consideration by the Competition Commission. Ivan Lewis, Labour's shadow culture secretary, accused Hunt of putting the *"perceived interests of his party and career ahead of the public interest"* in a Commons debate on the subject. Lewis said Hunt had given the pro-Tory News Corp the green light in the same week that he had named Lord Patten, a former chairman of the Conservative party, as the next chairman of the BBC Trust. *"This process has exposed an arrogant government, cavalier about its responsibility to be impartial and contemptuous of the importance of transparency in circumstances where there is a high level of public mistrust,"* he added. Source: Guardian.co.uk (3/2/11). Note: The author's references to News International & the issues mentioned above, preceded all knowledge of the phone-hacking scandal & the subsequent effect, which occurred just prior to going to print.

(204) - *"I don't want to see the military fall but rise to new heights, I want them to be heroes."* Spoken by **Aung San Suu Kyi** (b. 1945) to John Simpson of the BBC when interviewed on 14th November 2010

(205) - *". . I do not think that violence really pays - Violence begets more violence."* **Aung San Suu Kyi** (b. 1945), on release from house arrest, to the BBC's John Simpson (13/11/10).

(206) - *"I am for national understanding . . I believe in human rights & the rule of law . . I never hate another person or work for personal gain."* **Aung San Suu Kyi** (b. 1945) speech to supporters (14/11/10)

(207) - *"Aung San Suu Kyi is dedicated to the unification of all ethnicities and religious groups. Her revolution is one of the spirit and that means, as I understand her, including ALL aspects of the human heart and mind as natural to the whole. ALL beliefs. ALL persuasions. ALL religions. It also includes the many religious divisions within the military as well. She's a unifier. A healer. A builder of bridges. She does not harbor anger. Nor do her key colleagues. They are rooted in metta or loving-kindness."*
Alan Clements who wrote 'The Voice of Hope' (2007) - in dialogue with the author (4/3/11).

(209) - *"She is absolutely the one person who can unite everyone."* **Benjamin Rogers**, writer ('Than Shwe, Unmasking Burma's Tyrant' 2010) and political activist - in dialogue with the author (4/3/11)

(209) - *"It has been an uplifting and recurring surprise to me that - whether you are trying to stop war, species extinction, starvation, pollution, resource destruction, or simply providing clean water for all - the solution only requires a change in our mind-set, replace; greed with self control, apathy with action, and disrespect with a gentle caring for everybody and everything."* **Christ Darwin** (b. 1961) Great-great-grandson of Charles Darwin - writer, environmental conservationist & campaigner

POSTSCRIPT

(210) - *"Fifty years on, we may well ask ourselves, 'What has changed?'. We may well sadly conclude, 'not a lot'. But that would be to underestimate the progress of the world in these past 50 years . . "* **Kate Allen** (b. 1955), UK Director of Amnesty International, quoted in Amnesty Magazine (50 years Special Edition - May/June 2011)

(211) - *"There is a great and growing desire for change in the world; change that ushers in a renewed commitment to ethical and spiritual values, that resolves conflicts peaceably, employing dialogue and non-violence, that upholds human rights and human dignity as well as human responsibility."* **The Dalai Lama** (1935), 'Human Rights, Democracy & Freedom'; from Messages on his website: www.thedalailama.com.

(212) - *"This is the most peaceful time in history."* **Steven Pinker** (b. 1954) - 'On the Myth of Violence' (TED Lecture March 2007). According to Pinker, in the 20th century, there was spike in violence in the 1960s to 1980s but in 1950s an average of 65,000 deaths /p/conflict/p/y, going down to 2,000 d/p/c/p/y in 2000's

(213) - *"Today we are so interdependent, so closely interconnected with each other, that without a sense of universal responsibility, a feeling of universal brotherhood and sisterhood, and an understanding and belief that we really are part of one big human family, we cannot hope to overcome the dangers to our very existence - let alone bring about peace and happiness."* **The Dalai Lama** (1935), 'A Human Approach to Peace', from Messages on his website; www.thedalailama.com

(214) - From 'Perfect Hostage' (2007), by **Justin Wintle** (b. 1949)

(215) - *"Oh strange dreamer! You would change your ideas if you knew the heart of man as Philip knows it".* Libretto by Joseph Mery & Camille Du Locle for the opera 'Don Carlos' by Giuseppe Verdi (1884)

(216) - *"There were at least four rebel groups operating within the Karenni-controlled area (The Shan Democratic rebels, the KIA, the Muslim fighters & the Wa) . . all four groups were under the general, sometimes nominal, command of the National Democratic Front (NDF)":* 'From the Land of Green Ghosts' by **Pascal Khoo Thwe** (b. 1967), talking of around 1988.

(217) - NDF Website: www.ndf-burma.blogspot.com

(218) - *". . a force of protection rather than a force of destruction . . one could say that to maintain a professional, honourable, army would be an act of common sense."* Quoted by **Alan Clements** in 'The Voice of Hope' (2008)

(219) - *"I definitely support the approach of the NLD . . ASSK is an idealist but definitely not naive . . Though it is all very well for me to sit here and say so, real progress in Burma means action (non-violent) & as USSK has said herself it needs commitment & bravery. Though it is tough to say so, martyrs really help. Nelson Mandela & ASSK are very much 'martyrs' to their causes. Burma needs more action & yes, Gene Sharp's 198 Methods would be very useful. The 'Madres de Plaza de Mayo' made a real difference through their suffering & changed Argentina. Look at South America now, what a huge move forward towards civilisation." "Burma's 'Roadmap to Democracy' was a very good sign of this . . Violence in the world is in its death throws." "You don't know how insecure a government feels that is unelected."* From author's meeting with **John Simpson** (4/5/11)

(220) - *"Meditation has helped to strengthen me spiritually in order to follow the right path. Also for me, meditation is part of a way of life because what you do when you meditate is to learn to control your mind through developing awareness. This awareness carries on into everyday life. For me, that's one of the most practical benefits of meditation - my sense of awareness has become heightened. I'm now much less likely to do things carelessly and unconsciously."*
In conversation with **Alan Clements** - quoted in his book; 'The Voice of Hope' (2008)

(221) - *"It all comes down to violence. The kind of songs and music and films that you are talking about deal with violence in some form or other."* **Aung San Suu Kyi** (b. 1945).
From 'The Voice of Hope' (2008), by Alan Clements

(222) - *"When I despair, I remember that all through history, the way of truth and love have always won. There have been tyrants and murderers, and for a time they can seem invincible, but in the end they always fall. Think of it - always."* **Mohandas Gandhi** (1869-1948), quoted by Alan Clements in *'The Voice of Hope' (2008)*

(223) - *"there's never just one way in politics"* (Aung San Suu Kyi) *"Rather than force a showdown with the regime, she'd prefer take the long road"* (**John Simpson**), reported by the BBC Asia Pacific (20th June 2011)

(224) - *"I'm a fan of her values not her person, she is a metaphor for a non-local language beyond ethnicity and a great heroine of universal freedom but freedom is larger than Suu Kyi - a leader of universal revolution - the genie is out of the bottle. She doesn't need to leave Burma to travel the world."* The author in conversation with **Alan Clements** (30th May 2011)

(225) - *"Gandhi's teachings on non-violent civil resistance and the way in which he had put his theories into practice have become part of the working manual of those who would change authoritarian administrations through peaceful means. I was attracted to the way of non-violence, but not on moral grounds, as some believe. Only on practical political grounds."* **Aung San Suu Kyi** (b. 1945), quoted from her 2nd Reith Lecture (5/7/11)

(226) - For example, see 'Burma/Myanmar, What Everyone Needs To Know', Chapter 4, by **David I. Steinberg** (2010)

(227) - *" . . Gandhi's message lays the foundation for a renewed vision of nonviolence as an antidote to terrorism and unilateral politics in our world. . . According to Gandhi, the greatest moral duty was to fight the unjust even though it may cause us to suffer, because through our suffering we can show others the mistake they are making. Gandhi knew that violence unlike anger is not a natural phenomenon and it ultimately robs us of our humanity. Therefore he invited us to change our life style and our way of looking at things in order to be able to change the world. He said: "You must be the change you want to see in the world." The power of these words, spoken over 60 years ago, is often drowned out in the social and political violence of today's world. But Gandhi is probably the most important thinker whose precepts could guide the crisis-ridden world of 21st century . . "* **Dr. Ramin Jahanbegloo** (b. 1956) is an Iranian-Canadian philosopher, author of 20 books & the CEO of the Nonviolent Initiative for Democracy (NID). See: www.nidemocracy.org/en/publications/nonviolence-in-a-new-century

(228) - *"We should accept that we cannot impose democracy at the barrel of a gun; that we cannot drop democracy from 10,000 feet – and we shouldn't try"* **David Cameron,** British Prime Minister (b. 1966),

from a speech given in Islamabad (quoted by the Independent - 5th September 2008)

(229) - *"A hammer is sometimes required to pry dictators fingers off the window ledge of power"* **Kate Adie** (b. 1945), the renowned war correspondent & commentator, in conversation with the author.

(230) - *"I have learned that you cannot kill an ideology with a gun; vengeance begets more vengeance; jubilation at catching one so-called criminal doesn't further the ideals which I hope we are advocating in the world . . this is part of historical process, we're trying to stop people using the argument of pre-emptive strike right, to go out and kill people that disagree with them . . that premise should be challenged in a court of law . . it should be examined and we should know under what circumstances we can go to war. That is already governed by the UN Charter; we can only use armed force in self-defence or if approved by the security council of the UN."* **Ben Ferencz** (b. 1920). Chief Prosecutor for the US, Nuremberg Tribunal - quoted on the BBC's 'Newsnight', on 17th May 2011

(231) - *"When you think how fast the world has moved to multilateralism, and extend the graph onwards into the future, you can see how the old systems could well die out. The obvious examples are France and Germany, but there are so many others. Already, countries which think in purely self-centred ways seem a little old-fashioned".* **John Simpson** (b. 1944), in conversation with the author (23rd June 2011)

---

(232) - *"The time for the lone wolf is over. Gather yourselves! Banish the word struggle from your attitude and your vocabulary. All that we do now must be done in a sacred manner and in celebration. We are the ones we've been waiting for..."* Hopi Elder's Message - concluding the charter of 'Rights and Humanity' titled; 'Shining the Light - A Call for Action', available in full at; www.rightsandhumanityglc.org

Anthony Russell

INDEX I

Those Quoted

Afaqui, Aijaz (161) - "*. . my son, like thousands of other Muslim boys, spends hours blasting away at his own people .*" (in American video games such as; *'Muslim massacre'; 'War in the Gulf'; 'Conflict: Total Terror'*). Reported in News International (Karachi - Oct 2010)

Adie, Kate

(201) - "(Change in Burma), *will have to come from inside*"

(229) - "*A hammer is sometimes required to pry dictators fingers off the window ledge of power*"

Afaqui, Aijaz (168) - "*. . . my son, like thousands of other Muslim boys, spends hours blasting away at his own people .*" (in American video games such as; *"Muslim massacre"; "War in the Gulf"; "Conflict: Total Terror"*). reporting in News International (Karachi - Oct 2010)

Allen, Kate (210) - "*Fifty years on, we may well ask ourselves, 'What has changed?'. We may well sadly conclude, 'not a lot'. But that would be to underestimate the progress of the world in these past 50 years . . *"

Al-Sadat, Anwar (170) - "*. . . no one can build his happiness at the expense of the misery of others. . the call for permanent and just peace, based on respect for the UN resolutions, has now become the call of the whole world*"

Ashoka (195) - "*What have I done? If this is a victory, what's a defeat then? Is this a victory or a defeat? Is this justice or injustice? Is it gallantry or a rout? Is it valour to kill innocent children and women? Do I do it to widen the empire and for prosperity or to destroy the other's kingdom and splendour? One has lost her husband, someone else a father, someone a child, someone an unborn infant.... What's this debris of the* *corpses? Are these marks of victory or defeat? Are these vultures, crows, eagles the messengers of death or evil?"*

Arrow, Ruaridh (198) - *"One of the main points which we used was Sharp's idea of identifying a regime's pillars of support,"* he said. *"If we could build a relationship with the army, Mubarak's biggest pillar of support, to get them on our side, then we knew he would quickly be finished."*

Augustine, St

(15) - *"Where there is nothing, there is God"*

(134) - *"The just war"* laid out by in *"On the City of God"* (5th century AD) and taken up by Medieval thinkers such as Thomas Aquinas

Aung San Suu Kyi

(96) - *"I do not think that violence really pays . . violence begets more violence"*. was released from house arrest on 13th November 2010 and was interviewed by the BBC's John Simpson on 15th November. This was her first face-to-face interview for seven years. (112) - *"Real freedom means freedom from fear"*

(161) - *"The gun is always there for use . . . we are convinced that the non-violent approach is best"* (of M Ghandi) Aung San Suu Kyi is the Burmese pro-democracy opposition leader, who has spend over 14 years in prison or house arrest

(174) *"Without a revolution of the spirit, the forces which produced the iniquities of the old order would continue to be operative, posing a constant threat to the process of reform and regeneration. It is not enough merely to call for freedom, democracy and human rights. There has to be a united determination to persevere in the struggle, to make sacrifices in the name of enduring truths, to resist the corrupting influences of desire, ill will, ignorance and fear"*. (172) - *"It is not power that corrupts but fear. Fear of losing power corrupts those who wield it and fear of the scourge of power corrupts those who are subject to it."* from her speech "Freedom From Fear" (1990)

(180) - *"Thus to provide the people with the protective coolness of peace and security, rulers must observe the teachings of the Buddha. Central to these teachings are the concepts of truth, righteousness and loving kindness. It is government based on these very qualities that the people of Burma are seeking."*

(204) - *"I don't want to see the military fall but rise to new heights, I want them to be heroes."*

(205) - *". . I do not think that violence really pays - Violence begets more violence."*

(206) - *"I am for national understanding . . I believe in human rights & the rule of law . . I never hate another person or work for personal gain."*

(221) - *"It all comes down to violence. The kind of songs and music and films that you are talking about deal with violence in some form or other."*

(223) - *there's never just one way in politics"*

(125) - *"Gandhi's teachings on non-violent civil resistance and the way in which he had put his theories into practice have become part of the working manual of those who would change authoritarian administrations through peaceful means. I was attracted to the way of non-violence, but not on moral grounds, as some believe. Only on practical political grounds."*

(223) - *". . . a sufficiency of non-violent heat will melt the hardest heart."*

Aquinas, St. Thomas (135) - (1225-1274) wrote 'The Summa Theologica' (1265-1274). Aquinus was a 13th century theologian and philosopher, with great influence on the Christian Church

Barlow, Rich (82) - 'The British biologist and atheist (Prof. Richard Dawlins) believes that altruism in modern humans is essentially an evolutionary oops, albeit a beneficial one. It paid off in prehistory, when people lived in clans and protecting others meant the survival of their own gene pools; now that we've expanded into large cities, our instinct to help others still kicks in, even though those we aid may have no relation to us': (for the Richard Dawkins Foundation)

Baum, Lyman Frank (33) - *"Whenever I feel blue, I start breathing again".* (1856 - 1919); an American author of children's books, best known for writing The Wonderful Wizard of Oz.

Bodhidharma, The (4) - *"All know the way, but few actually walk it."*

Bold, Robert (118) - *"If might is right, then love has no place in the world. It may be so, it may be so. But I don't have the strength to live in a world like that".* Father Gabriel to Rodrigo, from the film "The Mission". (Screenplay)

Branson, Richard (121) - *"You fail if you don't try. If you try and you fail, yes, you'll have a few articles saying you've failed at something. But if you look at the history of American entrepreneurs, one thing I do know about them: An awful lot of them have tried and failed in the past and gone on to great things."*

Briley, John (71) - *"I am a Muslim and a Hindu and a Christian and a Jew and so are all of you."* From the film Ghandi (Screenplay by Briley) about the Indian political and spiritual leader (1869 - 1948).

Buddha, The (Siddhārtha Gautama)

(11) - *"the far shore, the subtle, the very difficult to see, the unaging, the stable, the undisintegrating, the unmanifest, the unproliferated, the peaceful, the deathless , the sublime, the auspicious, the secure, the destruction of craving, the wonderful, the amazing, the unailing, the unailing state, the unafflicted, dispassion, purity, freedom, the unadhesive, the island, the shelter, the asylum, the refuge..."*

(59) - *"Every human being is the author of his own health or disease"*

(75) - *"All that we are is the result of what we have thought. If a man speaks or acts with an evil thought, pain follows him. If a man speaks or acts with a pure thought, happiness follows him, like a shadow that never leaves him"*

(111) - *"Hatred does not cease by hatred, but only by love; this is the eternal rule"*

Camaron, David (228) - *"We should accept that we cannot impose democracy at the barrel of a gun; that we cannot drop democracy from 10,000 feet – and we shouldn't try"*

Capra, Fritjof (1) - *"Modern physics has shown that the rhythm of creation and destruction is not only manifest in the turn of the seasons and in the birth and death of all living creatures, but is also the very essence of inorganic matter,"* and that *"For the modern physicists, then, Shiva's dance is the dance of subatomic matter."*

Carlin, John (104) *"Forgiveness liberates the soul. It removes fear. That is why it is such a powerful weapon".* From the film 'Invictus'. Story based on the book *'Playing the Enemy'* (b.1956)

Carnegie, Andrew (164) - *"Si vis pacem para pacem".* = *"If you want peace, prepare for peace".* From The National Arbitration and Peace Congress of 1907, presided over by; *"These vast armaments on land*

and water are being defended as a means, not to wage war, but to prevent war... there is a safer way ... it requires only the consent and the good-will of the governments. Today they say ... If you want peace, prepare for war. This Congress says in behalf of the people: Si vis pacem, para pactum, if you want peace, agree to keep the peace". (For Original source, see Vegetius)

Carter, Howard (116) - *"The mystery of his life still eludes us, the shadows move but the dark never quite dispersed"*

Churchill, Sir Winston S

(8) - *". . . No one pretends that democracy is perfect or all-wise. Indeed, it has been said that democracy is the worst form of government except all those other forms that have been tried from time to time . . "*

(143) - *"From Stettin in the Baltic to Trieste in the Adriatic an iron curtain has descended across the continent"*

(194) - *"I feel so lonely without a war"*

Clements, Alan

(184) - *". . So non-violence to her is about love"*

(207) - *"Aung San Suu Kyi is dedicated to the unification of all ethnicities and religious groups. Her revolution is one of the spirit and that means, as I understand her, including ALL aspects of the human heart and mind as natural to the whole. ALL beliefs. ALL persuasions. ALL religions. It also includes the many religious divisions within the military as well. She's a unifier. A healer. A builder of bridges. She does not harbor anger. Nor do her key colleagues. They are rooted in metta or loving-kindness."*

(218) - *". . a force of protection rather than a force of destruction . . one could say that to maintain a professional, honourable, army would be an act of common sense."*

(220) - *"Meditation has helped to strengthen me spiritually in order to follow the right path. Also for me, meditation is part of a way of life because what you do when you meditate is to learn to control your mind through developing awareness. This awareness carries on into everyday life. For me, that's one of the most practical benefits of meditation - my sense of awareness has become heightened. I'm now much less likely to do things carelessly and unconsciously."*

(124) - *"I'm a fan of her values not her person, she is a metaphor for a non-local language beyond ethnicity and a great heroine of universal freedom but freedom is larger than Suu Kyi - a leader of universal revolution - the genie is out of the bottle. She doesn't need to leave Burma to travel the world."*

Dalai Lama, The

(41) - *"Sometimes one creates a dynamic impression by saying something, and sometimes one creates as significant an impression by remaining silent"*.

(45) - *"humanity needs all the world's religions to suit the ways of life, diverse spiritual needs, and inherited national traditions of individual human beings."* And he goes further; *"every major religion of the world - Buddhism, Christianity, Confucianism, Hinduism, Islam, Jainism, Judaism, Sikhism, Taoism, Zoroastrianism - has similar ideals of love, the same goal of benefiting humanity through spiritual practice, and the same effect of making their followers into better human beings."*

(51) - *"With realization of one's own potential and self-confidence in one's ability, one can build a better world"*.

(57) - *"In Tibet we say that many illnesses can be cured by the one medicine of love and compassion."*

(74) - *"A mind committed to compassion is like an overflowing reservoir - a constant source of energy, determination and kindness . . . The compassionate mind is like an elixir; it is capable of transforming bad situation into beneficial ones. Therefore, we should not limit our expressions of love and compassion to our family and friends. Nor is the compassion only the responsibility of clergy, health care and social workers. It is the necessary business of every part of the human community."*

(153) - *"War is like a fire in the human community, one whose fuel is living beings."* *"Since armies are legal, we feel that war is acceptable; in general, nobody feels that war is criminal or that accepting it is a criminal attitude. In fact, we have been brainwashed. War is neither glamorous nor attractive. It is monstrous. Its very nature is one of tragedy and suffering."* *"After the officer in charge have given beautiful explanations about the importance of the army, its discipline and the need to conquer the enemy, the rights of the great mass of soldiers are*

most entirely taken away. They are then compelled to forfeit their individual will, and, in the end, to sacrifice their lives. Moreover, once an army has become a powerful force, there is every risk that it will destroy the happiness of its own country. "

(189) - "It is ironic that the more serious problems emanate from the more industrially advanced societies. Science and technology have worked wonders in many fields, but the basic human problems remain. There is unprecedented literacy, yet this universal education does not seem to have fostered goodness, but only mental restlessness and discontent instead."

(211) - "There is a great and growing desire for change in the world; change that ushers in a renewed commitment to ethical and spiritual values, that resolves conflicts peaceably, employing dialogue and non-violence, that upholds human rights and human dignity as well as human responsibility."

(213) - "Today we are so interdependent, so closely interconnected with each other, that without a sense of universal responsibility, a feeling of universal brotherhood and sisterhood, and an understanding and belief that we really are part of one big human family, we cannot hope to overcome the dangers to our very existence - let alone bring about peace and happiness."

Darwin, Chris (209) - "It has been an uplifting and recurring surprise to me that - whether you are trying to stop war, species extinction, starvation, pollution, resource destruction, or simply providing clean water for all - the solution only requires a change in our mind-set, replace; greed with self control, apathy with action, and disrespect with a gentle caring for everybody and everything."

Douglas, Lloyd C (156) - "The greatest mistake ever made by Rome".

Edison, Thomas (122) - "Success is 10 percent inspiration and 90 percent perspiration."

Einstein, Albert (18) - "Imagination is more important than knowledge".

Elizabeth I, Queen (79) - "I have no desire to make windows into men's souls"

Elliot, T. S.

(85) - " . . . In order to arrive at what you do not know, You must go by a way which is the way of ignorance."

(151) - *"What branches grow out of this stony rubbish?" "April is the cruellest month, breeding lilacs out of the dead land, mixing memory and desire, stirring dull roots with spring rain."*

Ferencz, Ben (230) - *"I have learned that you cannot kill an ideology with a gun; vengeance begets more vengeance; jubilation at catching one so-called criminal doesn't further the ideals which I hope we are advocating in the world . . this is part of historical process, we're trying to stop people using the argument of pre-emptive strike right, to go out and kill people that disagree with them . . that premise should be challenged in a court of law . . it should be examined and we should know under what circumstances we can go to war. That is already governed by the UN Charter; we can only use armed force in self-defence or if approved by the security council of the UN."*

Fromm, Erich

(14) - *"People today are yearning for human beings who have wisdom and conviction and the courage to act according to their convictions."*

(27) - *"What the sources of property are does not matter; nor does possession impose any obligations on the property owner. The principle is: 'Where and how my property was acquired or what I do with it is nobody's business but my own; as long as I do not violate the law, my right is unrestricted and absolute."*

(28) - *"To maintain control over private property we need to use power to protect it from those who would take it from us, because they, like us, can never have enough; the desire to have private property produces the desire to use violence . . "*

(31) - *" . . until the conquest (of nature) has become more and more equivalent to destruction. Our sprit of conquest and hostility has blinded us to the fact that natural resources have their limit and can eventually be exhausted, and that nature will fight back against human rapaciousness."*

(36) - *". . sleep is the only proper situation for inactivity, the state of awakeness is one in which laziness should have no place". "The paradoxical situation with a vast number of people today, is that they are half asleep when awake and half awake when asleep or when they want to sleep"*

(40) - *"If one is after quick results, one never learns an art. Yet, for modern man, patience is as difficult to practice as discipline and concentration."*

(48) - *"Modern man thinks he loses something - time - when he does not do things quickly; yet he does not know what to do with the time he gains - except kill it."*

(80) *"Today, millions of people in America & Europe try to find contact with tradition and with teachers that can show them the way. But in large part the doctrines and teachers are either fraudulent or vitiated by the spirit of public relations ballyhoo, or mixed up with the financial or prestige interests of the respective gurus."*

(131) - *"Security, sense of identity and confidence based on faith in what one is, on one's need for relatedness, interest, love, solidarity with the world around us, instead on one's desire to have, to possess, to control the world, and thus become the slave of one's possessions*

(186) *"assumption was, that what was good for the "system", for big corporations, was good for man, as man was innately egotistic, selfish & greedy, therefore man was being "natural"*

(187) - *"We hesitate not at all at leaving our own descendants this plundered earth as their heritage"*

Frost, Robert (127) - *" . . I shall be telling this with a sigh, Somewhere ages and ages hence: Two roads diverged in a wood, and I, I took the one less travelled by, And that has made all the difference."*

Gandhi, Mohandas

(3) - *"We do not need to proselytise either by our speech or by our writing. We can only do so really with our lives. Let our lives be open books for all to study".*

(7) - *". . as soon as you remove the cobwebs of ignorance that surround it, (the truth) shines clear"*

(38) - *"Prayer is not an old woman's idle amusement. Properly understood and applied, it is the most potent instrument of action"*

(50) - *"Prayer is not an old woman's idle amusement. Properly understood and applied, it is the most potent instrument of action"*

(61) - *"Man should forget his anger before he lies down to sleep"*

(86) - *"An eye for an eye only ends up making the whole world blind."*

(90) - *"The weak can never forgive. Forgiveness is the attribute of the strong."*

(106) - *"The weak can never forgive. Forgiveness is the attribute of the strong."*

(119) - *"I suppose leadership at one time meant muscles; but today it means getting along with people."*

(126) - *"Strength does not come from physical capacity. It comes from an indomitable will"*

(162) *"Instead, why not leave India to her own resources and thereby gain a moral victory before the world and be saved the ignominy of a very probably disaster."*

(157) - *"Non-violence is the greatest force at the disposal of mankind. It is mightier than the mightiest weapon of destruction devised by the ingenuity of man."*

(167) *"For peace has its victories more glorious than those of war. The non-violent method would have meant no abject surrender. It would have confounded all modern tactics of war, indeed rendered them of no use."*

(171) *"Liberty and democracy become unholy when their hands are dyed red with innocent blood." "No one who believes in non-violence, as a creed, need, therefore, sit still . . I stress only one condition, namely, let our pledge of truth and non-violence as the only means for the attainment of (home rule) be faithfully kept."*

(183) - *"A small body of determined spirits fired by an unquenchable faith in their mission can alter the course of history."*

(199) - *"You saying that your culture and morals are in danger of being destroyed leads one to think that the reform movement in your country was only skin-deep . . . Blaming the wolf (Japan), would not help the sheep much. The sheep must learn not to fall into the clutches of the wolf"*

(200) - *"I suggest that at the end of the war, whichever way it ends, there will be no democracy left to represent democracy . . It is a warning that if nobody reads the writing on the wall, man will be reduced to the state of the beast, whom he is shaming by his manners."*

(198) - *". . . a sufficiency of non-violent heat will melt the hardest heart."*

(161-2) - *"A nation's culture resides in the hearts and in the soul of its people"*

(222) - *"When I despair, I remember that all through history, the way of truth and love have always won. There have been tyrants and murderers, and for a time they can seem invincible, but in the end they always fall. Think of it - always."*

Gardner, Howard (176) - *"The whole course of human development can be viewed as a continuing decline in egocentrism".*

Gibran, Kahlil (46) - *"You talk when you cease to be at peace with your thoughts"*

Goldsmith, Oliver (2) - *"Where wealth accumulates and men decay"*

Henley, William E (125) - *"Out of the night that covers me, Black as the pit from pole to pole, I thank whatever gods may be For my unconquerable soul. In the fell clutch of circumstance I have not winced nor cried aloud. Under the bludgeonings of chance My head is bloody, but unbowed. Beyond this place of wrath and tears Looms but the Horror of the shade, And yet the menace of the years Finds and shall find me unafraid. It matters not how strait the gate, How charged with punishments the scroll, I am the master of my fate: I am the captain of my soul*

Hindu Scriptures (66) - *"The vessel that gives for ever".* "Apshir Patra" (in Hindi) - notion of constant giving.

Hindu Scriptures (101) - *"naham vipro na ca nara-patir napi vaisyo na sudro naham varni na ca grha-patir no vanastho yatir va kintu prodyan nikhila-paramananda-purnamrtabdher gopi-bhartuh pada-kamalayor dasa-dasanudasah"* (Padyavali, 74):
"I am not a brahmana (priest or Vedic scholar), ksatriya (warrior or administrator), vaisya (agriculturalist or businessman), or sudra (worker), nor a brahmacari (celibate student), grhastha (householder), vanaprastha (renounced householder) or sannyasi (full renunciate). Being transcendental to this gross and subtle body, I am the servant of the servant of the servant of the lotus feet of the master of the gopis, Sri Krsna, who is the ultimate shelter of everyone, full of transcendental bliss and an ocean of unlimited nectar."- "trinad api Sunicena, taror api Sahisnuna, amanina manadena, kirtaniya sada hari" Translation: *"To be more humble then a blade of grass, to be more tolerant than a tree, Always give respect to others and expect none in return, In that state of mind one can chant the Holynames Constantly".*

Huxley, Aldous (196) - *". . . If any resistance is to be offered by the many to the few, it must be offered in a field in which technological superiority does not count . . . that (we) will be able to extort liberty from a ruling minority equipped by science with the very latest in self-propelled flame-throwers and atomic missiles seems in the highest degree unlikely. It is in satyagraha, or non-violent direct action, that the only hope of future revolutions resides."* And went on to say; *"The pen and the word are at least as mighty as the sword; for the sword is wielded in obedience to the spoken or written word."*

Jahanbegloo, Ramin (227) - *" . . Gandhi's message lays the foundation for a renewed vision of nonviolence as an antidote to terrorism and unilateral politics in our world. . . According to Gandhi, the greatest moral duty was to fight the unjust even though it may cause us to suffer, because through our suffering we can show others the mistake they are making. Gandhi knew that violence unlike anger is not a natural phenomenon and it ultimately robs us of our humanity. Therefore he invited us to change our life style and our way of looking at things in order to be able to change the world. He said: "You must be the change you want to see in the world." The power of these words, spoken over 60 years ago, is often drowned out in the social and political violence of today's world. But Gandhi is probably the most important thinker whose precepts could guide the crisis-ridden world of 21st century . . "*

Jesus Christ

(43) - *"Only in his home town, among his relatives and in his own house is a prophet without honour"* (NIV Bible) or "A prophet is not without honour, but in his own country, and among his own kin, and in his own house" (King James Bible)

(63) - *"But I say unto you, Love your enemies, bless them that curse you, do good to them that hate you, and pray for them which despitefully use you, and persecute you"* The New Testament, St James Bible; Mattew 5:44

(83) - *"To the Jews who had believed him, Jesus said, "If you hold to my teaching, you are really my disciples. Then you will know the truth, and the truth will set you free.",* quoted by St John the Evangelist 8:31

(154) - on Peace: *"But I say to you that hear, Love your enemies, do good to those who hate you, bless those who curse you, pray for those who*

abuse you. If you love those who love you, what credit is that to you? For even sinners love those who love them. And if you do good to those who do good to you, what credit is that to you? For even sinners do the same." Luke 6:27-32;

"Then Peter came up and said to him, "Lord, how often shall my brother sin against me, and I forgive him? As many as seven times?" Jesus said to him, "I do not say to you seven times, but seventy times seven..." Matt 18:21-22;

"Blessed are the meek, for they shall inherit the earth... Blessed are the merciful, for they shall obtain mercy... Blessed are the peacemakers, for they shall be called sons of God". Matt 5:5-9;

"Then Jesus said to him, "Put your sword back into its place; for those who live by the sword, die by the sword". Matt 26:52

(87) - "Judge not, that ye be not judged. For with what judgment ye judge, ye shall be judged: and with what measure ye mete, it shall be measured to you again. And why beholdest thou the mote that is in thy brother's eye, but considerest not the beam that is in thine own eye? Or how wilt thou say to thy brother, Let me pull out the mote out of thine eye; and, behold, a beam is in thine own eye? Thou hypocrite, first cast out the beam out of thine own eye; and then shalt thou see clearly to cast out the mote out of thy brother's eye. Matthew 7:1-5 (King James Version).

(147) - *"You have heard that it was said, 'An eye for an eye and a tooth for a tooth.' But I tell you, do not resist an evil person. If someone strikes you on the right cheek, turn to him the other also. And if someone wants to sue you and take your tunic, let him have your cloak as well. If someone forces you to go one mile, go with him two miles. Give to the one who asks you, and do not turn away from the one who wants to borrow from you."* quoted in the Gospel of St Matthew 5:38-42 (New International Version). Same doctrine and similar words in St Marks' Gospel (6:27-31 NIV)

(108) - *"People were bringing little children to Jesus for him to place his hands on them, but the disciples rebuked them. **14** When Jesus saw this, he was indignant. He said to them, "Let the little children come to me, and do not hinder them, for the kingdom of God belongs to such as these. **15** Truly I tell you, anyone who will not receive the kingdom of God like a little child will never enter it." **16** And he took the children*

in his arms, placed his hands on them and blessed them." Mark 10:13-16 (NIV)

James, William (16) - ". . *But if the religion of exclusive scientificism should ever succeed in suffocating all other appetites out of a nation's mind, and imbuing a whole race with the persuasion that simplicity and consistency demand a 'tabula rasa' to be made of every notion that does not form part of the 'soi-disant' scientific synthesis, that nation, that race, will just as surely go to ruin, and fall a prey to their more richly constituted neighbors, as the beasts of the field, as a whole, have fallen a prey to man.."*

Jefferson, Thomas (128) - *"I ask so much confidence only as may give firmness and effect to the legal administration of your affairs. I shall often go wrong through defect of judgment . . I ask your indulgence of my own errors, which will never be intentional . . "*

Kaliyphani

(84) - *"So, in the light of this vision, respect would mean seeing beyond the body (whether plant, animal, insect, human (black/white, young/old etc.)) to the real person who is the soul. That way you have tremendous respect for the equality and rights of every tiny creature as an eternal part or spark of the whole spirit (God). When you 'see' the soul you don't have to get caught up in judging anyone, or feeling better or worse than anyone."*

(109) - *"Forgiveness then becomes effortless; "Forgive them Lord, they know not what they do."* (Reference from New Testament - Luke 23:34) *. . . that is not condescending but spoken from a platform of real knowledge."*

Kennedy, J. F. (120) *"Let both sides explore what problems unite us instead of belabouring those problems which divide us."*

Khoo Thwe, Pascal (216) - *"There were at least four rebel groups operating within the Karenni-controlled area (The Shan Democratic rebels, the KIA, the Muslim fighters & the Wa) . . all four groups were under the general, sometimes nominal, command of the National Democratic Front (NDF)"*

King Jr., Martin Luther (179) - *"In the process of gaining our rightful place we must not be guilty of wrongful deeds. Let us not seek to satisfy our thirst for freedom by drinking from the cup of bitterness and hatred. We must ever conduct our struggle on the high plane of dignity and discipline. We must not allow our creative protest to degenerate into* *physical violence. Again and again we must rise to the majestic heights of meeting physical force with soul force"*

Koran, The
(53) - 30:60 *"Therefore have patience. God's promise is true. Let not those who disbelieve drive you to despair".*
(101) - al-Ma'idah 5:8. *"Never let your enmity for anyone lead you into the sin of deviating from justice. Always be just: that is closest to being God-fearing."*

Leigh, David (143) - *"Iraq war logs reveal 15,000 previously unlisted civilian deaths. Leaked Pentagon files contain records of more than 100,000 fatalities including 66,000 civilians."*

Lenin, V. I. (113) - *"Only the dictatorship of the proletariat and the poor peasants is capable of smashing the resistance of the capitalists . . Power to the Soviets - this is the only way to make further progress gradual, peaceful and smooth . . "*

Lerner, Rabbi (90) - *". . . We are first to acknowledge our "sins" against others, and then make reparations. In turn, we ask for forgiveness and it is expected that just as each of us hopes that others will forgive us, we are expected to forgive others for their sins against us. Thereafter, we can turn to our failures in our relationship with God. We are assured that if we are sincere in our repentance, then God will forgive us".*

Levins, Richard (17) - *" . . . But science also has had dramatic failures. The promises of understanding and progress have not been kept, and the application of science to human affairs has often done great harm. Public health institutions were caught by surprise by the resurgence of old diseases and the appearance of new ones. Modern planning has not given us more habitable cities. Industrial design for greater efficiency has not made work more humane but, instead, led to increased bodily stress, anxiety, overwork and unemployment. Pesticides increase pests, create new pest problems and contribute to the load of poison in our habitat. Antibiotics create new pathogens resistant to our drugs. Modern high-tech agronomy watches our soils disappearing. The green revolution did not eliminate hunger but increased the polarisation between rich and poor and the dependence of developing countries on imports. Scientific theories have even been put forth to justify inequality, racism, aggression and competitiveness . . . "*

Mandela, Nelson

(129) - *"As we are liberated from our own fear, our presence automatically liberates others."*

(169) - *"If you want to make peace with your enemy, you have to work with your enemy. Then he becomes your partner".*

Mandela, Nelson (123) - *"As we are liberated from our own fear, our presence automatically liberates others".*

Massie, Robert K (126) - *"I have learned that a strong man has no need of power & a weak man is destroyed by it"* (From film script)

Mishneh Tora (86) - *"It is forbidden to be obdurate and not allow yourself to be appeased. On the contrary, one should be easily pacified and find it difficult to become angry. When asked by an offender for forgiveness, one should forgive with a sincere mind and a willing spirit. . . forgiveness is natural to the seed of Israel."* (Teshuvah 2:10)

Mitchell, Tamsin (47) - *"We cannot burst other people's bubbles, only our own"*

Muhammad, The Prophet (88) - *". . . the Most Gracious, the Most Merciful, and the Most Beneficent" and is more merciful to His creatures than a mother to her child".*

Obama, Barak (165) - *" . . . For even as we celebrate tonight, we know the challenges that tomorrow will bring are the greatest of our lifetime - two wars, a planet in peril, the worst financial crisis in a century . . tonight we proved once more that the true strength of our nation comes not from the might of our arms or the scale of our wealth, but from the enduring power of our ideas; democracy, liberty, opportunity, and unyielding hope."*

Oppenheimer, Robert J (182) - *" . . . I think it is true to say that atomic weapons are a peril which affect everyone in the world, and in that sense a completely common problem . . I think that in order to handle this common problem there must be a complete sense of community responsibility . . the point I want to make, the one point I want to hammer home, is what an enormous change of spirit is involved. . . We cannot forget our dependence on our fellow men"*

Patten, George S. (178) - *". . . a real man will never let his fear of death overpower his honour, his sense of duty to his country and his innate manhood. Battle is the most magnificent competition in which a human being can indulge."*

Pinker, Steven (212) - *"This is the most peaceful time in history."*

Pope, Alexander (81) - *"a little knowledge is a dangerous thing"*

Rabelais, Francois (24) - *"Nature abhors a vacuum"*

Rogers, Benjamin (209) - *"She is absolutely the one person who can unite everyone."*

Russell, Bertrand (19) - *"Science may set limits to knowledge, but should not set limits to imagination."*

St Paul the Evangelist (43) - *"Whoever does not love does not know God, because God is love."*

Sassoon, Siegfried (150) - *'I am a soldier, convinced that I am acting on behalf of soldiers. I believe that this war, upon which I entered as a war of defence and liberation, has now become a war of aggression and conquest. I have seen and endured the sufferings of the troops, and I can no longer be a party to prolong those sufferings for ends which I believe to be evil and unjust. I am not protesting against the conduct of the war, but against the political errors and insincerities for which the fighting men are being sacrificed. On behalf of those who are suffering now I make this protest against the deception which is being practised on them. Also I believe that I may help to destroy the callous complacence with which the majority of those at home regard the continuance of agonies which they do not share, and which they have not sufficient imagination to realise.'*

Schama, Simon (20) - *" . . very many Dutch paintings . . filter the perception of the eye through the lens of moral sensibility"*

Selden, John (13) - *"Preachers say, 'Do as I say, not as I do.'"*

Scott-Peck, M (58) - *" . . . I would say that if you have a patient or a client who has some real difficulty, psychological difficulty, look for the problem in their thinking. There is some area where they are not thinking correctly."*

Schumacher E. F.

(10) *". . if economic thinking pervades the whole of society, even simple non economic values like beauty, health or cleanliness can survive only if they prove to be 'economic'"*

(29) - *"Economy as a content of life is a deadly illness, because infinite growth does not fit into a finite world. That economy should not be the content of life has been told to mankind by all the great teachers".*

(54) - *"Man is small, and, therefore, small is beautiful"*

"A Buddhist economist would consider this approach (belief in constant growth) excessively irrational: since consumption is merely a means to human well-being, the aim should be to obtain the maximum of well-being with the minimum of consumption . . . The less toil there is, the more time and strength is left for artistic creativity. Modern economics, on the other hand, considers consumption to be the sole end and purpose of all economic activity"

Schweitzer, Albert (30) - *"It is obvious to everybody that we are in a process of cultural self destruction. What is left is not secure any more". "For two or three centuries many individuals have lived only as working beings and not as human beings."*

Scott-Peck, M. (54) - *" . . I would say that if you have a patient or a client who has some real difficulty, psychological difficulty, look for the problem in their thinking. There is some area where they are not thinking correctly. "*

Scriabin, Alexander (37) - *"In love's godlike breathing, there's the innermost aspect of the universe".*

Shakespeare, W. (71) - *"My bounty is as boundless as the sea, my love as deep. The more I give to these the more I have, for both are infinite".*

Shelden, John (13) - *"Preachers say, 'Do as I say, not as I do.'"*

Simpson, John (219) - *"I definitely support the approach of the NLD . . ASSK is an idealist but definitely not naive . . Though it is all very well for me to sit here and say so, real progress in Burma means action (non-violent) & as USSK has said herself it needs commitment & bravery. Though it is tough to say so, martyrs really help. Nelson Mandela & ASSK are very much 'martyrs' to their causes. Burma needs more action & yes, Gene Sharp's 198 Methods would be very useful. The 'Madres de Plaza de Mayo' made a real difference through their suffering & changed Argentina. Look at South America now, what a huge move forward towards civilisation." "Burma's 'Roadmap to Democracy' was a very good sign of this . . Violence in the world is in its death throws." "You don't know how insecure a government feels that is unelected."*

(231) - *"When you think how fast the world has moved to multilateralism, and extend the graph onwards into the future, you can see how the old*

systems could well die out. The obvious examples are France and Germany, but there are so many others. Already, countries which think in purely self-centred ways seem a little old-fashioned"

Smith, J.W. (163) - "*Estimates for the total casualties of the war vary, because many deaths went unrecorded. Most suggest that some 60 million people died in the war, including about 20 million soldiers and 40 million civilians. Many civilians died because of decease, starvation, massacre, bombing and deliberate genocide. The Soviet Union lost around 27 million people during the war, almost half of all World War II deaths. One of every four Soviet citizens was killed or wounded in that war*". (from "The World's Wasted Wealth 2, Save our Wealth, Save our Environment"

Tacitus (a) - "*They rob, kill & rape and call this 'Roman Rule'. They create a desert called 'Peace'*"

Tavener, Sir John

(22) - "*but I'm not interested in substance, it's the essence of the music that counts!*"

(44) - "*God reveals Himself through his 'theophanies', whether it be through Christ, the Buddha, or virgin nature or in the word made book, The Koran. Gods shows himself in everything that lives and this includes the sublime language of music.*"

(103) - "*The Roman Church will tell you, if you do this you'll go there, if you do that you'll go someplace else. It feels as if you're arriving at Heathrow Airport. But we don't know the judgment of God - no-one knows*"

(190) - "*(Sees us in) the grips of a global catastrophe, a global nightmare . . The ordinary people out there - there is something missing in their lives, they can't articulate exactly what it is, but they are searching.*" "*Having in our minds desanctified ourselves, we have also desanctified the natural world in our minds. This self-image and world view have their origin in our loss of memory, in our forgetfulness of who we are, and in our fall to a level of ignorance and stupidity that threatens the survival of our race.*"

Taylor, Jack (152) - "*When you're young, it sounds exciting, war; shooting people. It's not exciting at all, it's a dirty business*"

Tefila Zaka (85) - *"I know that there is no one so righteous that they have not wronged another, financially or physically, through deed or speech. This pains my heart within me, because wrongs between humans and their fellow are not atoned by Yom Kippur, until the wronged one is appeased. Because of this, my heart breaks within me, and my bones tremble; for even the day of death does not atone for such sins. Therefore I prostrate and beg before You, to have mercy on me, and grant me grace, compassion, and mercy in Your eyes and in the eyes of all people. For behold, I forgive with a final and resolved forgiveness anyone who has wronged me, whether in person or property, even if they slandered me, or spread falsehoods against me. So I release anyone who has injured me either in person or in property, or has committed any manner of sin that one may commit against another [except for legally enforceable business obligations, and except for someone who has deliberately harmed me with the thought 'I can harm him because he will forgive me']. Except for these two, I fully and finally forgive everyone; may no one be punished because of me. And just as I forgive everyone, so may You grant me grace in the eyes of others, that they too forgive me absolutely."* Closing of the *Tefila Zaka* meditation, recited before Yom Kippur

Teresa, Mother (of Calcutta)

(32) - *"We need to find God, and he cannot be found in noise and restlessness. God is the friend of silence. See how nature - trees, flowers, grass- grows in silence; see the stars, the moon and the sun, how they move in silence... We need silence to be able to touch souls."*

(118) - *"Do not wait for leaders; do it alone, person to person"*

(104) - *"If you judge people, you have no time to love them."*

(124) - *"Do not wait for leaders; do it alone, person to person."*

(133) - *"Peace starts with a smile"*

(134) - *"Every time you smile at someone, it is an action of love, a gift to that person, a beautiful thing"*

Twain, Mark (78) - *"To know a man you must know his history"*

UNICEF (141) - *"Land-mines are uniquely savage in the history of modern conventional warfare not only because of their appalling individual impact, but also their long-term social and economic destruction (Ms. Machel) . . . Children in at least 68 countries are today threatened by* *what may be the most toxic pollution facing mankind — the contamination by mines of the land they live on. Over 110 million land-mines of various types — plus millions more unexploded bombs, shells and grenades — remain hidden around the world, waiting to be triggered by the innocent and unsuspecting, the report says. Once laid, a mine may remain active for up to 50 years. Unless vigorous action is taken, mines placed today will still be killing and maiming people well into the middle of the next century. In just one district of Viet Nam 300 children have died, 42 have lost one or more limbs, and 16 have been blinded as a result of land-mines laid during the Viet Nam war. As one Khmer Rouge general put it, a land-mine is the most excellent of soldiers, for it is "ever courageous, never sleeps, never misses."*

Vaknik, Dr Sam (52) - *"Primary Narcissism, in psychology is a defence mechanism, common in the formative years (6 months to 6 years old). It is intended to shield the infant and toddler from the inevitable hurt and fears involved in the individuation-separation phase of personal development. . . The term narcissism was first used in relation to human psychology by Sigmund Freud after the figure of Narcissus in Greek mythology"*

Vegetius, Flavius Renatus (159) - *"If you want peace, prepare for war."*

Wiesel, Elie (181) - *"What will the legacy of this vanishing century be? . . Surely it will be judged, and judged severely in both moral and metaphysical terms . .So much violence, so much indifference".*

Williams, Dr Rowan (142) - *"One of the aspects of traditional just war theory is that you need to know what would count as a good end and how you would know when you have that and what to do then . . . I don't think we had that in place sadly. I don't think we knew what we would do next or what would count as our ending. And that is the tragedy"*

Well, H. G. (146) *"The war to end all wars"*

Yeats, W.B. (15) - *"we shall not come to that joy, that battle, till we have put out the senses, everything that can be seen and handled, as I put out this candle. (He puts out candle). We must put out the whole world as I put out this candle (puts out another candle). We must put out the light of the stars and the light of the sun and the light of the moon* (puts out the rest of the candles), *till we have brought everything to nothing once again. I saw in a broken vision, but now all is clear to me. Where there is nothing, where there is nothing - there is God!*"

"Peace is more than merely an absence of war, violence or conflict. If children die of hunger or malnutrition, if people do not have homes to live in, if the sick have to go without treatment, if people commit crime and are not punished, peace cannot be said to prevail. If the people do not have an opportunity to decide how they are going to be ruled and who are going to rule them, if they do not have freedom of thought and freedom of speech, if they are subject to the whims of the military or a dictator, there is no peace worth the name. Peace is pointless if the people are not free and happy. They must have every opportunity to lead, without hindrance, the kind of life they wish to"

SHEIKH HASINA, PRIME MINISTER OF BANGLADESH

INDEX II

Subject Matter